Srila Prabhupada:
The Story of Abhay Charan De

Srila Prabhupada:
The Story of Abhay Charan De

by Sthita-dhi-muni dasa

illustrations by
Amala Chaitanya dasa
Yadupriya devi dasi
Puskara dasa

IVS
INSTITUTE FOR VAISHNAVA STUDIES
Gainesville, Florida

We wish to express our deep appreciation
to Satsvarupa dasa Goswami and
the Bhaktivedanta Book Trust
for writing and publishing
the *Srila Prabhupada-lilamrta*,
upon which this story is based.

The cover picture of "Young Abhay performing Rathayatra"
has been used with permission from the
Bhaktivedanta Book Trust International © 1980.
Chota Books also gratefully acknowledges the BBT
for the use of various direct quotes from the
Srila Prabhupada-lilamrta. All such materials are
© Bhaktivedanta Book Trust International, Inc.

Copyright © 2016 by S. E. Kreitzer

ISBN 978-0-9981871-3-6

Persons interested in the subject matter of this book
are invited to correspond with:

ivspublishing@gmail.com

Institute for Vaishnava Studies (IVS)
PO Box 1791
Alachua, FL 32616

Contents

1. Born in Calcutta **1**
2. Abhay's Father and Mother **7**
3. Rathayatra in Abhay's Neighborhood **13**
4. School Days and Growing Up **17**
5. Scottish Churches' College **22**
6. Marriage and a Career **25**
7. Srila Bhaktisiddhanta Sarasvati **27**
8. Life in Allahabad **31**
9. Family Life and Spiritual Life **33**
10. Abhay Begins His Mission **38**
11. Jhansi and the League of Devotees **41**
12. Alone **44**
13. Getting Ready **47**
14. Coming to America **51**

15. A Newcomer to a New Land   57

16. New York City   61

17. The Bowery   64

18. A New Start on Second Avenue   69

19. The First Hare Krishna Temple   72
    in America

20. The Swami's First Followers   77

21. Initiations   81

22. Chanting Hare Krishna   86

23. The Hare Krishna Explosion   91

24. Prabhupada's Victory   99
    a poem by Kalakantha dasa

Glossary   103

BRITISH INDIA 1896

- Delhi
- Ganges
- Yamuna
- Vrndavan
- Jansi
- Allahabad
- Ganges
- BENGAL
- Mayapur
- Calcutta
- Jaganatha Puri
- Bombay

ARABIAN SEA

BAY OF BENGAL

Ceylon (Sri Lanka)

1

Born in Calcutta

It is 1896, and Queen Victoria of England rules over India. Her British Empire is the largest in the world, and India is her most important colony.

Every year toward the end of summer, millions of people are out in the streets celebrating Janmastami, the festival of Lord Krishna's birthday. Devotees are everywhere visiting temples, friends, and family. In Calcutta, even the Muslims and British take part in the fun. Most of India stays up well past midnight enjoying the celebration.

The next day, after all is quiet, Rajani and Gour Mohan De's son is born. As it is the custom for a new mother to deliver her child at the home of her own mother, the infant is born at his grandmother's house along the Ganges River.

Because the child is born on a holiday that Nanda Maharaja celebrated thousands of years earlier for baby Krishna, the boy's uncle wants to call him Nandulal—but his parents have another idea. They name him Abhay Charan, meaning "one who is fearless, having taken shelter at Lord Krishna's lotus feet."

Rajani and Gour Mohan want their son to become a Vaishnava, a devotee of Lord Krishna. A few days after Abhay's birth, the new family returns home to their apartment in Calcutta.

Many parents in India invite an astrologer to predict their baby's future. Abhay's astrologer predicts that he will travel across the ocean when he is seventy years old, become an important teacher of religion, and open 108 temples. Everyone is amazed by what the astrologer says.

In Calcutta, Abhay's family lives in an apartment at 151 Harrison Road. In this neighborhood most of the people wear traditional Indian clothes like dhotis and saris. Abhay's wealthy cousin Lokanath Mullik owns not only Abhay's building, but a number of the other neighborhood shops and buildings, where many of Abhay's other cousins live.

Across the street from Abhay's home is the Mullik's Radha-Govinda temple. Many generations of Mulliks have worshiped Radha-Govinda and supported the temple with money earned from their neighborhood shops.

In the morning, Abhay's cousins visit the temple Deities. They bring Them vegetable dishes, rice, and *kachauris*, and then offer Radha-Govinda's *prasadam* to the numerous guests who visit the temple during the day.

Sometimes little Abhay visits the Deities in his baby carriage. Later, when Abhay grows up to be known as Srila Prabhupada, he tells his disciples stories about when he was a young boy in India:

"I used to ride in the same baby carriage with my cousin Siddhesvar Mullik. He used to call me Moti, and his nickname was Subidhi. A servant would push us together. If one day my cousin did not see me, he would become mad. He would not go in the baby carriage without me. We would not separate even for a moment."

If Abhay's mother and father are busy, a servant minds the two small boys, often taking them to visit the temple. First he carefully pushes them in their baby carriage across busy and noisy Harrison Road, filled with people, bicycles, and horse-drawn carriages. He then steers the boys under the trees and through a gateway in the red sandstone walls surrounding the temple. Another metal gateway leads to the Deities' courtyard, where two large stone lions with raised front paws sit as if guarding Their Lordships. The courtyard is filled with the peaceful sound of cooing pigeons and chirping sparrows. The temple guests often look inside the carriage and play with the little boys who have come to visit Radha-Govinda.

The servant then pushes the carriage past a statue of Garuda, Vishnu's faithful eagle servant. Finally, within the innermost courtyard, they see Radha-Govinda. The Deities stand on a raised platform surrounded by tall, stone pillars supporting a large, stone roof. Abhay and Subidhi hold hands as they toddle close to Their Lordships' altar.

Srila Prabhupada later recalled: "I can remember standing at the doorway of the temple saying prayers to Radha-Govinda. We would watch for hours together. The Deity was so beautiful, with His slanted eyes."

The Radha-Govinda Deities are made of polished brass and are eighteen inches tall. They are beautifully dressed in silver crowns, jewelry, and silk clothes. Krishna wears a dhoti and vest, and Radharani wears a sari. Everyday after the *pujaris* bathe and

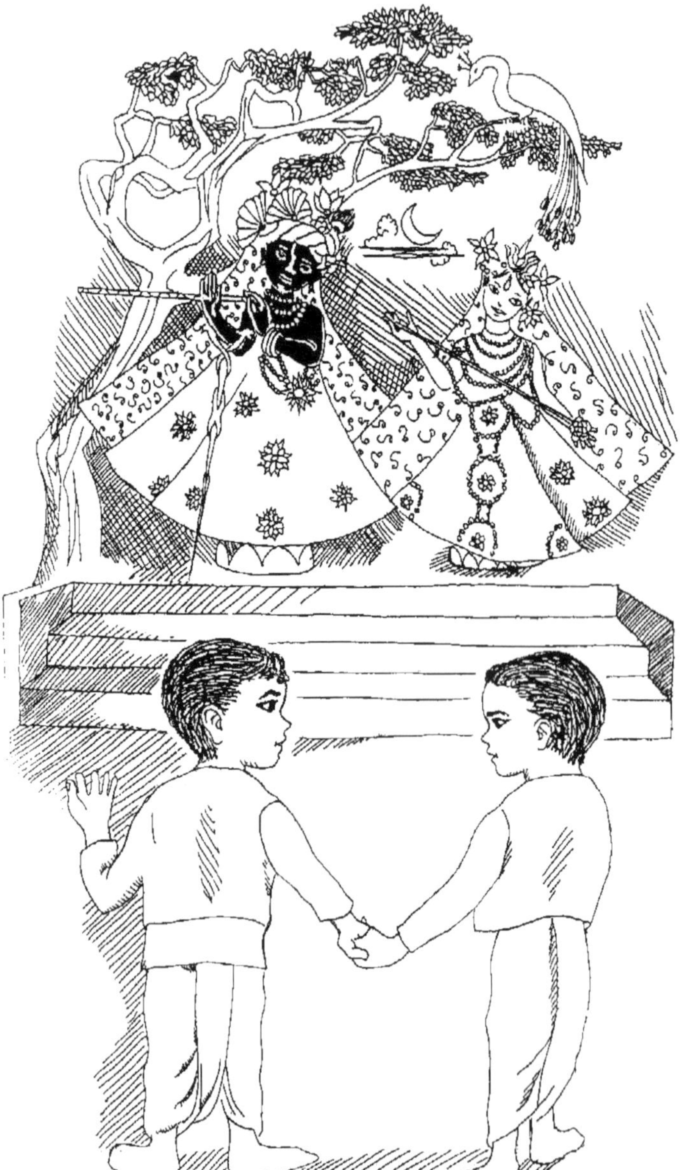

dress the Deities, they decorate Radha-Govinda with fresh, fragrant flowers.

Little Abhay loves watching the beautiful forms of Radha-Govinda standing under Their silver canopy and throne decorated with fresh flowers. To Abhay, They appear as if They are dancing before Their devotees.

Birds chirp in the courtyard as the guests come and go. Sometimes a devotee starts a *kirtan*, chanting Hare Krishna while others play drums and *kartals*. Abhay and his cousin watch the *pujaris* offer Radha-Govinda incense, a ghee lamp, flowers, and a peacock fan, one after another. When the *arati* ceremony is over, a *pujari* blows a conch shell.

When Abhay is one-and-a-half years old, he becomes seriously ill with typhoid fever. The family doctor advises his father to give him chicken soup, but Abhay's father is against the idea. "No, I cannot allow it. We are not meat-eaters. We do not cook chicken in our kitchen."

The doctor is afraid that Abhay will die. "Don't mind," he says, "I shall make it at my house and bring it in a jar."

"All right, but only if it is necessary for my son to live," replies Gour Mohan.

When the doctor returns with the chicken soup medicine, he tries to get Abhay to drink it. But Abhay refuses—he vomits instead.

"All right," the doctor says, "Never mind, this is no good."

Gour Mohan throws the soup away. By Krishna's grace, Abhay gets better without it.

When Abhay is three, while playing with matches in front of his house, one of the matches lights and catches his clothes on fire. Fortunately, a man passing by smothers the flames. Abhay is okay, but he gets a small scar on his leg.

When Abhay is four, a dangerous disease called "the plague" attacks Calcutta. Dozens of people die every day and thousands leave the city. To counteract this plague, an elderly devotee steps forward and organizes a large Hare Krishna chanting party to travel throughout the city. When the party reaches Abhay's neighborhood, he wants to join. He enjoys chanting and dancing to the Hare Krishna mantra. Fortunately, everyone in Abhay's family stays healthy, and soon the plague leaves Calcutta.

2

Abhay's Mother and Father

Abhay's father, Gour Mohan De, is a Vaishnava devotee of Lord Krishna. He raises his son to be a devotee, just as his own parents raised him.

Gour Mohan is a quiet, peaceful man, earning his living as a cloth merchant. In the evening, when he locks his shop up for the day, he places a bowl of rice in the middle of the floor. This way, at night the hungry neighborhood rats eat the rice and leave the cloth alone.

After Gour Mohan returns home, he reads from the *Chaitanya-churitamrita* and the *Srimad-Bhagavatam*, two important Vaishnava scriptures. He also chants Hare Krishna on his *japa* beads and worships his Deities.

Gour Mohan is a gentle, friendly man who does not like to punish his son. If ever Abhay needs to be corrected, Gour Mohan first apologizes by saying, "You are my son, so now I must correct you. It is my duty. Even Chaitanya Mahaprabhu's father would correct Him. So please do not mind."

Gour Mohan and Abhay enjoy the time they often spend together. They like taking long walks, sometimes at the beach.

Though Abhay's family does not own much, they wear nice clothes and have plenty of food. Abhay's father often invites four or five dinner guests for *prasadam*.

Many years later Srila Prabhupada tells his disciples, "We were happy—not that because we did not purchase a motorcar we were unhappy. My father used to say, 'God has ten hands. If He wants to take away from you, with your two hands how much can you protect? And when He wants to give to you with His ten hands, with two hands how much can you take?'"

Gour Mohan encourages Abhay to become a serious devotee able to teach Krishna consciousness to others. Whenever Vaishnavas visit Gour Mohan's home, he asks them, "Please bless my son so that Srimati Radharani will bless him to become a devotee of Krishna."

He also wants Abhay to learn to play the *mridanga* drum used in *kirtans* by the devotees. When little Abhay begins taking *mridanga* lessons, his hands can barely reach both ends of the drum at the same time. Watching his young son learn Vaishnava music makes Gour Mohan happy.

When some of Abhay's uncles suggest that Abhay should grow up to study law in England, Gour Mohan is against the idea. He tells them he doesn't want his son to go away and develop bad habits just to earn money.

Abhay is the pet child of both of his parents. Along with nicknames such as Moti, Nandulal, Nandu, and Kocha, his grandmother also calls him Kachauri-muhki because he loves to eat *kachauris*. *Kachauris* are spicy, fried pastries stuffed with *dal*

beans. His grandmother and mother make *kachauris* for him, which he loves to keep in his vest pockets. Abhay also watches the street peddlers make *kachauris* at their roadside stands. Sometimes they give him some, and sometimes he gets them from neighbors. Abhay's vest pockets often bulge with *kachauris*.

Once, when his mother will not make him *kachauris*, Abhay becomes so angry that she has to send him to bed early. When Gour Mohan returns home he asks, "Where is Abhay?"

Rajani explains that Abhay has been naughty, but Gour Mohan says, "No, we should make them for him." He wakes his son and makes *kachauris* for everyone.

Gour Mohan likes seeing his son get whatever he needs. Once, when Abhay asks for a toy gun in the marketplace, his father says no. The little boy begins to cry.

"All right, all right," Gour Mohan says, and buys him the gun.

But then Abhay wants two guns.

"You already have one! Why do you want another one?"

"One for each hand," cries Abhay. He lies down in the street, crying and kicking his legs. Gour Mohan again gives in, affectionately buying his son the second gun, making naughty Abhay a happy boy.

Abhay's mother, Rajani, also comes from a family of devotees, just like her husband. She is thirty when her son is born. While her husband is softhearted, Rajani is strong-minded. She is a religious woman who cares deeply for her family.

Rajani often performs little rituals that she feels will protect Abhay from danger. Whenever he goes outside to play, Abhay's mother touches his forehead with her finger. Though Abhay does not understand what it means, he trusts his mother in every way.

One day Rajani puts an iron bangle on his leg for protection. When Abhay's friends ask why he is wearing a bangle, he feels strange. He goes back to his mother and demands, "Open this bangle!"

"I will do it later."

Abhay cries, "No, now!"

Once Abhay swallows a watermelon seed. When his friends tell him that it will grow a watermelon inside his belly, little Abhay becomes afraid and runs to his mother. She says, "Don't worry, I will chant a mantra to protect you."

Srila Prabhupada later said, "Mother Yasoda would chant mantras in the morning to protect Krishna from all dangers throughout the day. When Krishna killed some demon, she thought it was her chanting that protected Him. My mother would do a similar thing with me."

Srila Prabhupada admitted, "I was very naughty when I was a boy. I would break anything. When I was angry, I would break things which my father kept for our guests. Once my mother was trying to bathe me and I refused. I knocked my head on the ground so hard that blood came out."

Though Abhay is often naughty, he remains completely dependent on his mother. If she accidentally puts his shirt on backwards, he wears it and doesn't say a thing. He trusts her about everything. Although he is stubborn, he feels safe with his mother.

Sometimes Abhay's family travels to his uncle's village, where in the evening everyone comes together to hear stories from the *Ramayana* and *Mahabharata* about Rama and Krishna. They listen with the other villagers, and as they return home they talk about the wonderful stories they've just heard. When Abhay gets tucked into bed, he falls asleep dreaming about Krishna.

Abhay likes to play with his sister Bhavatarini. They often go together to Radha-Govinda's temple to see Their Lordships. If ever they have a problem, they pray to God for help. They ask Him, "Please, Krishna, help us fly this kite."

Besides his two toy guns, Abhay likes playing with a wind-up car, a cow that jumps when a rubber ball is squeezed, and a dancing toy dog that the family doctor gave him when he was sick. Sometimes Abhay likes to pretend that he is a doctor too. He gives "medicine" to his friends, but it is only dust.

3

Rathayatra in Abhay's Neighborhood

Every year, Abhay loves to go to Lord Jagannatha's Rathayatra festival in Calcutta. While the festival is celebrated in many Indian cities, the biggest festival is held in Jagannatha Puri, where for thousands of years many hundreds of thousands of people have pulled the three large, wooden carts on the two-mile parade.

A different Deity rides on each cart. The first cart carries Lord Jagannatha, who is Krishna. On the second is Lady Subhadra, Krishna's younger sister. Krishna's older brother, Lord Balarama, rides on the last cart. Each cart is about forty-five feet tall, colorfully painted, and decorated with flags and a high canopy.

Gour Mohan tells Abhay how four hundred years earlier, Lord Chaitanya and His friends joyfully danced and chanted Hare Krishna in front of Lord Jagannatha's Rathayatra cart. As Lord Chaitanya, Krishna behaved just like a devotee in order to teach people the chanting of Hare Krishna. Sometimes Abhay looks at the railroad schedule wondering how much it would cost to visit Jagannatha Puri.

In Calcutta, the Mulliks organize a large Rathayatra festival. Their parade begins in front of the Radha-Govinda temple, and the chariots are pulled up and down Harrison Road. After the parade, Abhay's cousins serve a huge feast.

Abhay is inspired to have his own Rathayatra festival. He asks his father to help. Together they visit several carpenter shops, but they find that building a new cart will cost too much money. Abhay cries in disappointment. As they walk home, an old woman stops and asks Gour Mohan why the boy is so upset. Gour Mohan explains that his son wants to start a Rathayatra festival but they can't afford to build a cart.

"Oh!" says the woman, "I have a cart!"

She invites Abhay and his father to see it. It is just the perfect size, about three feet tall. Though it is old, it can be repaired, and Gour Mohan buys it.

Together, Gour Mohan and Abhay paint and decorate the little Rathayatra chariot. They place a canopy on top of the sixteen wooden columns so that it looks just like the carts in Jagannatha Puri. They even place a wooden horse and driver on the front. Abhay wants everything just right; he is very excited. He even wants to make his own fireworks, but Rajani says no, it is too dangerous.

Abhay gets his friends to help, especially his sister Bhavatarini. His friends' mothers also agree to help cook a feast for Abhay's Rathayatra festival.

Abhay carefully copies whatever he sees the grown-ups do. First he makes sure the Deities are beautifully dressed and offered nice food. Abhay offers Them *arati* with a ghee lamp and incense. The other children bow down, offering their obeisances to Lord Jagannatha.

Many cousins, aunts, and uncles join the children's Rathayatra parade. Abhay leads the chanting and dancing while his friends play drums and *kartals*. At the end of the parade, the little cart rolls through the gates of Radha-Govinda's temple, and everyone stands in front of the Deities with folded hands.

Some of Gour Mohan's friends joke, "Why haven't you invited us? You are holding a big festival, and you don't invite us? What is this?"

"They are just children playing," Gour Mohan tells them.

"Oh, children playing?" the men continue to joke. "Now you are telling us this is only for children?"

Abhay's festival lasts eight days, just like in Jagannatha Puri. Every day Abhay happily takes Lord Jagannatha's Rathayatra cart on parade, and Gour Mohan spends money so Rajani can cook a feast and offer flowers to the Deities. While the festival is great fun for the neighborhood children, for Abhay it is a serious event. Each year he eagerly looks forward to holding a special children's Rathayatra festival for Lord Jagannatha.

Ever since he was a baby, Abhay has watched his father worshiping Radha-Krishna at home, and the *pujaris* worshiping Radha-Govinda at the temple. He wonders, "When will I be able to worship Krishna like this?"

When he is six, Abhay asks his father for his own Deities. Gour Mohan agrees, and gets Abhay his own little Radha and Krishna. Both Abhay and Bhavatarini enjoy worshiping these small Deities. They dress Them, and sometimes chant and sing *bhajans* to Them. Abhay offers his food to his Deities before he eats. He also offers Them incense and a ghee lamp and puts Them to bed at night, just like his father and the priests do at the Radha-Govinda temple.

Sometimes Abhay's and Bhavatarini's older brothers and sisters tease them. They laugh and say, "If you want to live a long time you should be studying rather than worshiping your Deity." But Abhay and Bhavatarini say they don't care.

4

School Days and Growing Up

Abhay is old enough now to go to school, but he has other ideas. "Why should I go?" he considers. "I will play all day."

When Rajani tells Gour Mohan, Abhay knows his father won't be angry. He tells his father, "I shall go tomorrow."

"All right, he will go tomorrow," says Gour Mohan. "That's all right."

But the next morning, Abhay claims he feels sick, and his father lets him stay home another day.

It worries Rajani that her son is missing school. She pays a man named Damodara to bring Abhay, but when Damodara takes him to his teacher, Abhay tries to run away. Damodara catches Abhay and carries him back to school. After a few days, Abhay finally decides to go on his own.

Fortunately, Abhay quickly becomes an attentive and well-behaved student. Starting when he is five and lasting until he is eight, a teacher comes to his home and teaches him Sanskrit and Bengali after school.

When he is eight, Abhay goes to Mutty Lall Seal Free School. It is on the corner of Harrison and Central Road, not far from his home. It is a boys' school, started by a rich Vaishnava family many years earlier. The teachers are Indian and all the students come from devotee families.

Dressed in dhotis and *kurtas*, small groups of neighborhood children walk to school carrying books and lunch boxes. The children talk and play inside the walls surrounding the white stone school building. When the bell rings, the boys rush through the halls and up the stairs to the second floor, where the teachers gather them into their classrooms.

The boys sit behind long wooden desks where they learn math, science, history, and geography, as well as their own traditional Vaishnava culture. In front of each student on the desk sits an old-fashioned pen and inkwell.

The teachers are strict and the students must pay careful attention. If the boys are caught being naughty, they must stand on the bench behind their desks.

The children read from a book called *Folk Tales from Bengal*. Bengal is the state in India that Calcutta is part of. The book tells mysterious stories of witches, ghosts, and talking animals, along with stories of princes and princesses, heroic warriors, saintly *brahmanas* (and sometimes wicked ones), and clever thieves. There are tales of noble and virtuous marriages, as well as stories of saints who give up everything for spiritual life.

When Abhay turns ten, workers lay trolley tracks along Harrison Road. Amazed, Abhay watches the first streetcars ride the rails. A large wire on top of each trolley touches an electric cable stretching high above the tracks. Abhay imagines that he can touch the cable with a stick and race along the train tracks like a streetcar.

In those days, electric power is a brand new invention, and only the very rich have it in their homes. Soon the city government replaces the old, gas street lamps with electric lights that burn a carbon-tipped light bulb. Now and then workers need to climb the poles to change these carbon tips. Abhay and his friends love to collect the old tips left on the ground by the workers.

Another new invention at this time is a gramophone box, an old-fashioned machine that works something like a CD player. When Abhay hears a gramophone box playing for the first time, he thinks maybe a little electric man, or possibly even a ghost, is singing inside.

At school, Abhay plays goalie for the soccer team. He also likes to ride his bicycle along Calcutta's busy streets. His favorite ride is to Dalhousie Square, where there are large spraying fountains, and the British governor's mansion, which can be seen through large gates.

He also rides through Maidan Park among beautiful stretches of flat, green land filled with large trees and stately buildings. Abhay sees the race track, the sports stadium, and Fort William. The Ganges River borders the park, and sometimes he rides along its banks. Here there are many temples and bathing ghats with stone steps leading to the river.

Gour Mohan often invites holy men, called sadhus, to his home for lunch. Even though they often appear to be only beggars, or even drug users, Gour Mohan is always respectful. Sometimes among these guests are real holy men, and Abhay learns many important things by listening to his father speak with these sadhus.

When Abhay is twelve, he hears a story about a yogi who is asked by his guru, "What do you want to eat?"

The yogi requests, "Fresh pomegranates from Afghanistan."

"All right," the guru answers. "Go into the next room." There the yogi finds a fresh branch full of ripe pomegranates.

Though Abhay hears many stories of magical yogic tricks, it does not sound important when compared to the devotional life taught by his father. To Abhay, spiritual life means worshiping Radha and Krishna, and holding a Rathayatra festival.

When Abhay is fifteen, he falls sick with a disease called beriberi, which makes his legs swell. Every day his mother rubs his legs with a special medicine, and Abhay soon gets well.

But a year later, Rajani suddenly passes away. Abhay somehow feels that now his childhood has ended. His mother's death affects his sisters even more. Fortunately, they still have their affectionate father to look after them. He helps them understand that the soul lives on even after the material body is finished. Krishna is everyone's best friend, and nothing happens unless He allows it. Gour Mohan explains that even though there are times when life feels painful, Krishna always has everyone's best interest at heart.

5

Scottish Churches' College

In 1914 World War I begins. England and Germany are enemies in the battle, and many Indians join the British to help fight the Germans. Abhay watches the English warplanes land on the racetrack in Maidan Park. Two years later he begins college.

While Gour Mohan wants his son to become educated so that he can responsibly take care of a family, he also wants Abhay to keep the pure habits of a Vaishnava. Gour Mohan therefore avoids sending Abhay away to school in England.

Calcutta has two important colleges. One school, Scottish Churches' College, was started many years earlier by a Christian minister. Along with economics, philosophy, English literature, and Sanskrit, the students learn the Christian Bible. Since Scottish Churches' is not far from Harrison Road, Abhay attends college there.

While some of the teachers are Indians, most are British. Srila Prabhupada later remembered them in a friendly way: "We respected our professors as our fathers. The relationship between the students and the professors was very good. The assistant principal was a perfect and kind-hearted gentleman with whom we sometimes joked."

In college, Abhay likes playing goalie for the soccer team. He also performs in a school play about Lord Chaitanya. In the drama, Abhay is Advaita Acarya.

Abhay spends most of his day either in class or studying. He finds he doesn't have time to worship his Radha-Krishna Deities, so he carefully puts Them in a box. But a year later he has an unusual dream. Abhay's Krishna Deity appears before him and complains, "Why have you put Me away in this box? You should take Me out and worship Me again." Abhay feels he is not properly caring for his Deities, so he again takes up Their worship.

During Abhay's college days, many students are disturbed by the way the British rule their country. They feel that the British disrespect them by claiming that Indians aren't experienced enough to govern their own nation. The students begin holding secret meetings to discuss the problem of foreign rule.

While Abhay isn't deeply concerned about who governs India, he knows that the British believe Krishna consciousness to be something unimportant. However, the other college students speak of a time when, after the foreigners leave, Indians will rule their own country, and then the world will take both India and her ancient Vedic culture seriously. This idea attracts Abhay.

One of the most important leaders of India's Independence movement is Mahatma Gandhi, and he asks the students not to accept a British college diploma when they graduate. He claims that these schools are teaching Indians to depend on outsiders and not think for themselves. Gandhi preaches that refusing a diploma is a nonviolent way to protest the British government.

Abhay will soon be ready for graduation. He thinks seriously about what Gandhi has said. Although he passes his final exams in 1920, he does not accept his diploma.

6

Marriage and a Career

While Abhay attends college, Gour Mohan feels that soon his son will need a family of his own. In India, parents often follow the Vedic tradition of arranging marriages for their children. Gour Mohan knows many families in Calcutta with nice daughters. After careful thought, he decides that Radharani Datta might be a good wife for Abhay. Gour Mohan and Radharani Datta's family meet and agree that it is a good choice.

Normally before a young couple marries, they remain living separately at home with their parents while gradually getting to know each other. Abhay visits Radharani at her parent's home, where she sometimes cooks dinner for Abhay and her family.

Though Abhay appreciates that Radharani is an attractive girl from a good family, he has an idea to marry someone else. When Gour Mohan learns about this, he tells Abhay that marrying an ideal wife may not be everything. While a good marriage and family life is important, the best consideration is for a strong devotional life. Gour Mohan advises, "If you understand this, your spiritual life will be easier later on."

Abhay considers his father's idea. He loves his father and wants to please him, appreciating Gour Mohan's concern for his spiritual advancement. In the end, he decides to make the best of the marriage arrangements made by his father.

While a college degree would give Abhay many fine career opportunities, he refuses to accept a diploma. In those days, most Indians considered it highly honorable to reject a British college diploma. Still, Abhay needs a job.

Gour Mohan's friend and family doctor, Dr. Kartick Bose, has a large laboratory that makes drugs, soaps, and other medical supplies. Dr. Bose knows that Abhay is an intelligent boy, and thinks of him as a son. He offers him a job at his medical laboratory.

7

Meeting Srila Bhaktisiddhanta Sarasvati

One day a friend of Abhay, named Narendranath Mullik, invites him to visit a saintly person whom he recently met at a nearby ashram.

Abhay says, "Oh, no! I know all these sadhus. I'm not going." He remembers the many so-called sadhus often invited by his father to his home for dinner.

Naren replies, "This sadhu is a genuine, saintly devotee. Srila Bhaktisiddhanta Sarasvati is his name, and he is a great follower of Lord Chaitanya." Abhay agrees to go with Naren.

The two friends walk through the crowded Calcutta streets filled with people, horses and buggies, oxcarts, motor taxis, and buses. When they reach the ashram, a young man recognizes Naren and invites them upstairs to the second-floor rooftop where Srila Bhaktisiddhanta Sarasvati is speaking to a group of devotees and guests.

Bhaktisiddhanta Sarasvati sits straight and tall. He is slender, with a fair, golden complexion. While he wears glasses and looks scholarly, he also appears strong and bold. As Abhay and Naren know he is a Vaishnava *sannyasi*, they immediately offer him their respectful obeisances.

Once the two young men find a place to sit, Srila Bhaktisiddhanta tells them, "You are educated young men. Why don't you preach Lord Chaitanya Mahaprabhu's message throughout the whole world?"

Abhay doesn't know what to say. This is the first time he has met this *sannyasi*, and already Srila Bhaktisiddhanta is asking him to dedicate his life to Lord Chaitanya.

As Abhay listens to Bhaktisiddhanta Sarasvati speak, he senses that this sadhu is a special devotee. He feels that Srila Bhaktisiddhanta cares deeply about serving Chaitanya Mahaprabhu's mission of spreading Krishna consciousness. Abhay is attracted by Bhaktisiddhanta Sarasvati's strong convictions. He feels humbled and inspired. Abhay wants to hear more, yet he has a doubt.

"Who will hear your Chaitanya's message?" Abhay challenges. "We are a dependent country. First India must become independent. How can we spread Indian culture if we are under British rule?"

In a calm, deep voice, Srila Bhaktisiddhanta responds, "Krishna consciousness does not need to wait for a change in Indian politics. It does not matter who rules the country. Krishna consciousness is so important and special that it cannot wait."

Abhay is moved by the boldness of Bhaktisiddhanta Sarasvati's words. While the whole country is talking about forcing the British to leave, Srila Bhaktisiddhanta Sarasvati makes the claim that such concerns are unimportant.

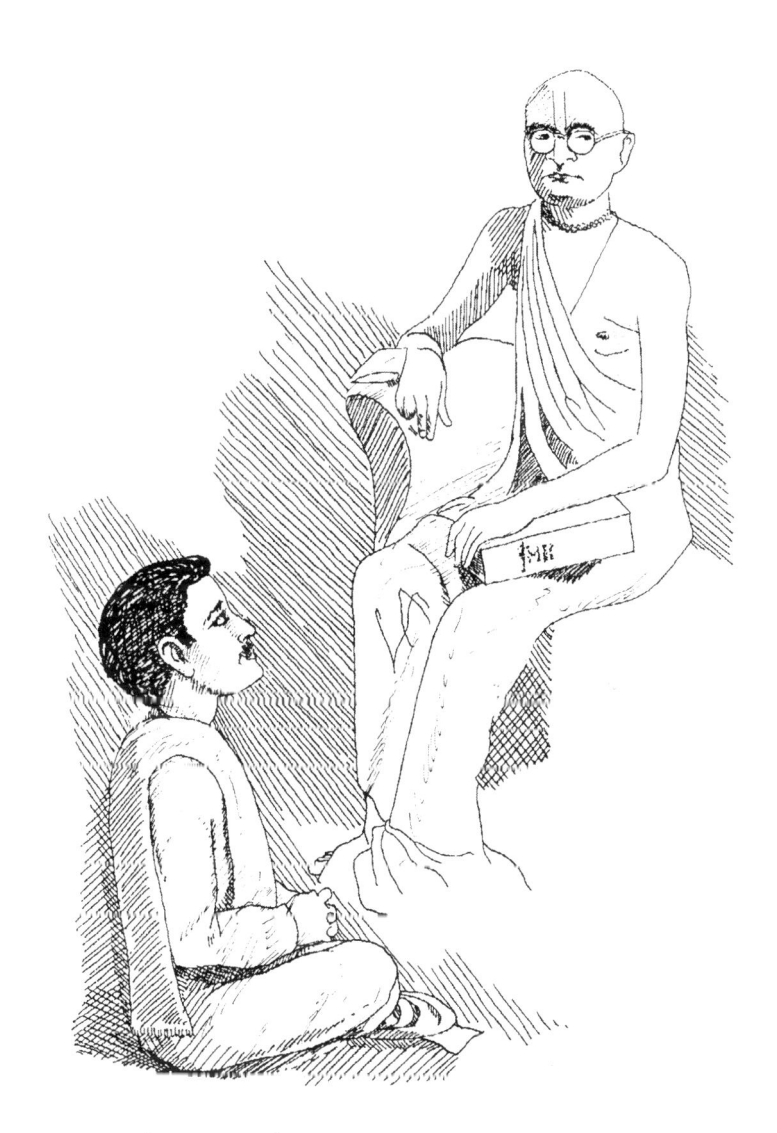

Srila Bhaktisiddhanta goes on to explain how even with a different government, people still need to take care of what is most important. Even though leaders may change, the ongoing problems of material life will nonetheless remain. Lasting happiness will be found only when we reawaken our eternal relationship with the Supreme Personality of Godhead. That is the mission of Lord Chaitanya Mahaprabhu.

As a Vaishnava, Abhay appreciates the wisdom of these words. It reminds him of the things he learned in his childhood from his father. After hearing Srila Bhaktisiddhanta, Abhay's feelings grow stronger in his heart.

When Abhay and his friend walk home that night, Naren asks, "So, Abhay, what was your impression? What do you think of him?"

"He is wonderful!" Abhay responds. "The message of Lord Chaitanya is in the hands of a very expert person."

Later in life, Srila Prabhupada described to his disciples his first meeting with his spiritual master, Srila Bhaktisiddhanta: "I was from a Vaishnava family, so I could appreciate what he was preaching. Of course, he was speaking to everyone, but he found something in me. And I was convinced by his argument and mode of presentation. I was so struck with wonder. I could understand: Here is the proper person who can give a real religious idea. . . . I was thinking that I had met a very nice saintly person."

8

Life in Allahabad

Abhay enjoys spending time with members of Srila Bhaktisiddhanta Sarasvati's movement, the Gaudiya Math. His followers have over sixty-four temples in India. They print and distribute large quantities of Krishna conscious books, and hold festivals for the public. Abhay wants to help them as much as he can.

In 1923, Abhay and Radharani move with their baby son to a town called Allahabad. There, Abhay sets up a medical supply business. Abhay wants to earn money not only for his own family, but also to help Srila Bhaktisiddhanta's followers spread Krishna consciousness.

Abhay's new business is called Prayag Pharmacy. His friend Dr. Ghosh becomes his business partner. At the pharmacy, Dr. Ghosh treats patients and Abhay sells medicine. Abhay also travels by train throughout northern India, selling medical supplies to hospitals, doctors, and other drugstores. For many years his business prospers.

In 1928, some of Srila Bhaktisiddhanta Sarasvati's Gaudiya Math followers come to Allahabad to start a preaching center. They ask Abhay if he can help.

"Yes, I will help you," he enthusiastically responds. He wants to do whatever he can. Soon a center is started just a short walk from his home. Abhay likes spending time with the Allahabad devotees. Gour Mohan, who lives with Abhay's family, also feels happy that these Vaishnavas have their temple close by.

By 1930 Gour Mohan has become an old man. He wonders how much longer he will live. One day he asks Abhay to donate their cow and calf to the Gaudiya Math devotees. He asks him to invite these Vaishnavas to their home for *prasadam* and Hare Krishna *kirtan*. That night, not long after the devotees leave, Gour Mohan passes away.

Abhay now feels as if he has just lost his dearest protector and well-wisher. All throughout his life his father carefully guided and treated him like a special person. It was Gour Mohan who constantly prayed to every holy man that he ever met to please bless his son to become a great devotee of Srimati Radharani.

Abhay feels shaken, but in his heart his father's kindness and instructions live on.

9

Family Life and Spiritual Life

Abhay's family continues to grow. Now he has two young sons and a daughter. Although he often needs to work in the pharmacy, he also enjoys spending time with his family.

Pacha is the nickname of one of Abhay's sons, and he is a mischievous little boy. Sometimes the neighbors tease him by saying, "If you sit down silently for one minute, I will give you a gift." But Pacha can never do it.

There is a table fan in Abhay's house, and Pacha wants to touch the spinning blade. Abhay warns, "No, no, don't touch." But Pacha does not want to listen.

Someone suggests "Just lower the speed and let him touch it."

So Abhay unplugs the fan and lets his son stick his finger in. When the slowly spinning fan hits Pacha's finger it makes a loud noise—TUNC. The little boy cries, but he isn't hurt; and he never tries it again.

Abhay's little girl is named Sulakshman. Abhay loves teaching her Vaishnava songs as she learns to speak.

Abhay often needs to travel to sell his medical supplies. Sometimes things go well and Abhay makes plans to use his money in Krishna's service. However, there are other times when he is not so successful. Yet Abhay sees everything as Krishna's arrangement.

In 1932, Abhay travels to Vrindavan to be with Srila Bhaktisiddhanta Sarasvati and his Gaudiya Math followers. They are leading a large group of devotees on a *parikram* to visit the different holy places. On *parikram* Srila Bhaktisiddhanta gives many lectures. Abhay takes every opportunity to listen to his spiritual master speak. He stays to hear every word.

A month later in Allahabad, the Gaudiya Math devotees buy land on which they plan to build a temple. Bhaktisiddhanta Sarasvati promises to come and lead a festival for the new temple's construction. He also wants to hold an initiation ceremony. Abhay asks the temple president if Srila Bhaktisiddhanta Sarasvati might consider offering him *harinam*, or "first" initiation.

When Bhaktisiddhanta Sarasvati arrives, he meets the devotees who wish to become his new disciples. Abhay offers his respect with folded hands.

Srila Bhaktisiddhanta remembers Abhay from Vrindavan. He looks pleased and tells the temple president, "Yes, he likes to hear. He does not go away. I have marked him. I will accept him as my disciple."

Bhaktisiddhanta Sarasvati gives Abhay both first and second initiation at the same time. Usually new disciples need to wait before receiving second initiation, but Srila Bhaktisiddhanta feels Abhay is ready to worship the Deities as a second-initiated *brahmana*.

At the time of initiation, the spiritual master awards his disciple a devotional name. Abhay Charan is now called Abhay Charanaravinda, meaning "fearless at Krishna's lotus feet."

Abhay's sister and brother attend the initiation ceremony; they know how important it is to him. But Radharani does not come. While she thinks it is nice that her husband wants to become a disciple of Srila Bhaktisiddhanta Sarasvati, it is not something she considers for herself.

Srila Prabhupada later described his marriage relationship: "My wife was a devotee of Krishna, but she had some other idea. Her idea was just to worship the Deity at home and live peacefully. My idea was preaching."

As the years go by, Abhay looks forward to meeting his spiritual master whenever he can. He also enjoys helping his Godbrothers at the Gaudiya Math serve their guru-maharaja, Srila Bhaktisiddhanta Sarasvati.

Whenever they are together, Bhaktisiddhanta Sarasvati always treats Abhay kindly. Sometimes when Srila Bhaktisiddhanta is chanting the Hare Krishna mantra on his *japa* beads, Abhay walks alongside chanting with him.

In November 1935, Abhay and his son travel to Vrindavan to be with Bhaktisiddhanta Sarasvati at Radha-kunda. When they arrive, Srila Bhaktisiddhanta gives the young boy a small *bandhi* jacket as a present.

Srila Bhaktisiddhanta Sarasvati then speaks about the Gaudiya Math's beautiful marble temple in Calcutta. Unfortunately, some of his leading disciples are fighting over which rooms they each want to use. They are competing to see who will be considered the most important devotee. Srila Bhaktisiddhanta feels that this is a serious problem.

Srila Bhaktisiddhanta confides in Abhay, "When we were living in a rented house we were happier.

But since we have been given this marble palace, there is friction between our men: 'Who will occupy this room? Who will occupy that room?' It would be better to take the marble from the walls and secure money to print books."

Srila Bhaktisiddhanta Sarasvati then looks at Abhay and says, "I have a desire to print some books. If you ever get money, *print books.*"

In 1936, Abhay sends a letter to his spiritual master asking, "Is there any particular service I can do?"

Two weeks later, Srila Bhaktisiddhanta writes back:

"I am fully confident that you can explain in English our thoughts and arguments to the people who are not conversant with the languages of the other members. That will do much good to yourself as well as your audience."

Abhay now understands the order of his gurumaharaja. It is the same instruction he was given when they first met in 1922.

Not long after, Srila Bhaktisiddhanta Sarasvati passes away, leaving this material world. Again Abhay feels the deep loss of a most valuable well-wisher, but he also feels confident knowing what Srila Bhaktisiddhanta Sarasvati wants him to do. This helps Abhay feel close to his spiritual master. Srila Bhaktisiddhanta Sarasvati desires that he teach Krishna consciousness around the world. He wants Abhay to preach in the English language.

10

Abhay Begins His Mission

Though Srila Bhaktisiddhanta Sarasvati left clear instructions about how to keep his movement organized, the Gaudiya Math leaders unfortunately find it difficult working together. Eventually, most of the temples split off from each other and try to spread Krishna consciousness as best they can on their own.

At the same time, Abhay's medical business is not going well. While he earns enough to take care of his family, he does not have extra money to help the Gaudiya Math.

Abhay turns his attention to writing and preaching with his Godbrothers. He becomes well known among the devotees for his classes and *kirtans*. In Bombay he helps to open a temple and to publish books.

In 1944, Abhay decides to print his own Krishna conscious magazine called *Back to Godhead*. In it he writes essays on Krishna consciousness, as well as devotional commentaries on world events in the news. It is not an easy project to do alone, especially as he has little money to spare. Also, because of

World War II paper is scarce, but somehow Abhay finds what he needs to print. He sells his magazine to people in the city streets and busy marketplaces. It is difficult, but Abhay is able to produce and distribute two issues.

After the war, England finally awards India her independence. Around this time, Abhay has a dream about his spiritual master. In it Srila Bhaktisiddhanta Sarasvati asks Abhay to leave home and take *sannyas*, the renounced order of life. As a *sannyasi* Abhay would be able to dedicate all his time to preaching.

Abhay wakes up a bit scared—this is not an ordinary dream. Still, he does not feel that the time is right to take up the austere life of a *sannyasi*.

Abhay is now fifty years old. Although his children are grown up, they do not seem ready to help him, even in business. And his wife does not understand his desire to serve his spiritual master in Krishna consciousness.

ABhay continues to write. One wealthy businessman offers to print his translation of the *Bhagavad-gita*, but Abhay cannot find his manuscript anywhere. No one in his family knows what happened to it.

Some of Abhay's Godbrothers print a magazine called *Gaudiya Patrika*. They ask him to write articles for it, which Abhay is happy to do. Sometimes, when he has a little money, he also prints his own magazine, *Back to Godhead*.

Whenever Abhay returns from his business travels, he invites friends to his home for *prasadam* and to discuss Krishna consciousness. He wishes that his wife and grown children would join him, but they prefer to stay upstairs.

11

Jhansi and The League of Devotees

Abhay regularly sells medical supplies to Dr. Sastri, one of his customers in the town of Jhansi. The doctor likes reading Abhay's *Back to Godhead* magazine, and feels that many other people in town will also enjoy hearing him speak. He arranges for Abhay to give a lecture on Krishna consciousness.

Many students from a local college attend Abhay's program. A number of doctors and local businessmen also come. They like his lecture and invite him to speak more often. Naturally, Abhay is encouraged by their enthusiasm.

Abhay cannot forget his experience in Jhansi when he returns home to his family. He wants to go back and preach full time. Abhay decides to hand over the management of his business to his son and nephew.

Back in Jhansi, Abhay makes new friends, who want to help him succeed. They consider him a serious devotee, and enjoy hearing him speak about

Krishna consciousness. Abhay visits their homes, leads *kirtans*, and gives *Bhagavad-gita* classes.

One day while on a walk, Abhay notices some empty buildings that look like a good place to open a preaching center. His friends contact the owner, and Abhay gets permission to move in.

Sometimes Abhay organizes a *harinam* party with as many as fifty people. They walk through Jhansi's streets chanting Hare Krishna, and when they return to their new center, Abhay gives a *Bhagavad-gita* lecture. They call themselves the League of Devotees.

Abhay and his friends hold an official opening celebration for the League. Many important people from Jhansi attend, and the local newspaper writes a favorable story about the new group of devotees.

While Abhay preaches in Jhansi and the surrounding villages, he also dreams of spreading Krishna consciousness around the world. He can't forget his spiritual master's ambitions.

One day the owner of the building asks Abhay to buy it for 5,000 rupees, but that is too much money for the Jhansi devotees. Abhay decides to return to Allahabad to try to raise the money there.

As before, when Abhay returns home, he invites friends to come over to chant and speak about Krishna. But his wife and family still prefer to stay upstairs drinking tea.

One day, Abhay cannot find his *Srimad-Bhagavatam*. He asks Radharani if she has seen it. She replies that she has sold it at the market to buy tea biscuits. Abhay is shocked. How could his wife trade his worshipable *Bhagavatam* for tea biscuits? Now he is certain. There is no hope that Radharani and his family will appreciate what Krishna consciousness means to him. For them, it is something you do at home—if it is easy.

Abhay is now fifty-seven, and his children are old enough to take care of their mother. There seems to be little more that he can do. If he wants to go forward and preach Lord Chaitanya's message on the order of his spiritual master, he will have to do it alone.

Abhay leaves home and goes to a Godbrother's ashram nearby. This time he feels certain that he will not return. Abhay stays a few days thinking over his decision, giving evening *Bhagavad-gita* classes, and chanting. Although he has no money and little help, he feels that he must somehow preach Krishna consciousness. This becomes his only business.

His friends in Jhansi are glad when he returns, but they also have problems. The owner of the building now wants to sell it to someone else. While Abhay and his friends want to keep the building for the League of Devotees, they have no money.

Abhay is disappointed, but there is little he can do. He could try to fight the owners in court, but that would mean a long legal battle, and he would rather preach Krishna consciousness. He decides it would be better to accept an invitation to help a Godbrother in Vrindavan. His Jhansi friends are sad when he leaves, but Abhay encourages them to keep everything going as best they can. He tells them that they can write him, but he realizes that Jhansi will not be the place to start a movement.

12

Alone

Abhay spends time living at different ashrams belonging to his Godbrothers, helping them spread Krishna consciousness. While Abhay still wants to preach Krishna consciousness in English around the world, his Godbrothers do not seem to share in his ambition.

Abhay begins to travel again. He goes to the homes of different well-wishers, where he chants and gives classes on Krishna consciousness. Sometimes he is invited to lecture at religious festivals. Abhay desires to write and publish books, and to start a group of serious full-time devotees who are inspired to spread Krishna consciousness around the world.

Abhay struggles to raise money to continue printing *Back to Godhead* magazine. He often stays in Vrindavan, the holy land of Krishna's birth, where he writes articles. As soon as he is able to raise enough money, he prints and then distributes *Back to Godhead* in the crowded cities of Bombay and Delhi. Not everyone is interested, yet he feels that he is doing something important.

Now in his sixties, Abhay is determined more than ever to try any idea that might help people come to Krishna consciousness. Although many express interest, few have time to give to Abhay's cause.

In modern India, people want to copy the ways of the Western countries such as Great Britain and America. Abhay remembers Srila Bhaktisiddhanta's instructions to preach Krishna consciousness around the world in the English language. If the Westerners take to Krishna consciousness, then India may better realize the importance of her own culture.

One night, Abhay again dreams of Bhaktisiddhanta Sarasvati asking him to take *sannyas*. Becoming a *sannyasi* means spending all of one's time preaching Krishna consciousness on behalf of the spiritual master and Lord Chaitanya. Many years earlier, Abhay felt afraid when he first had this dream. Now at sixty-three years old, he knows that the time is right.

Abhay talks to his Godbrother Bhaktiprajnana Kesava Maharaja about *sannyas*. He explains his desire to go to America and preach on behalf of their spiritual master, Srila Bhaktisiddhanta Sarasvati. Kesava Maharaja encourages him. He offers Abhay *sannyas* initiation in the year 1959.

Kesava Maharaja leads the initiation ceremony. As a *sannyasi*, Abhay is now called Bhaktivedanta Swami. *Swami* means "one who is in control of his senses," while *bhakti* means "devotion," and *vedanta* means "the end of knowledge."

As a *sannyasi*, Abhay is recognized as someone completely committed to teaching spiritual life. As Bhaktivedanta Swami, he can now dedicate his entire life to preaching the message of Chaitanya Mahaprabhu: to reawaken and develop one's natural love for Lord Sri Krishna, the Supreme Personality of Godhead.

13

Getting Ready

In Vrindavan, Bhaktivedanta Swami keeps a room at the Radha Damodara temple. There he writes and becomes inspired to bring Krishna consciousness to the West. He also rents a room at another temple in New Delhi, where he prints *Back to Godhead* and preaches. He often travels back and forth on a three-hour train ride.

One day a librarian suggests it might be better to print books. He notices that after people read a magazine or newspaper, they throw it away, but everyone keeps books because they are more permanent. Bhaktivedanta Swami likes this idea.

He decides to begin by translating *Srimad-Bhagavatam* into English. It is a long scripture explaining the devotional science of Krishna consciousness. Bhaktivedanta Swami feels that even if he cannot complete it, it will still be valuable. Then when he goes to the West, he'll have an important scripture from which to teach.

Although Bhaktivedanta Swami still teaches Krishna consciousness, he now spends much of his time translating *Srimad-Bhagavatam*. First, he studies the teachings of the great Vaishnava spiritual masters from the past. He translates into English what they originally wrote in Sanskrit, adding purports to explain the verses to a modern audience.

In 1962, Bhaktivedanta Swami gets a donation from a wealthy Indian businessman to print an English edition of the *Srimad-Bhagavatam*. He begins printing in Delhi. Every day he visits the printers, making sure that the book is coming out nicely.

It takes about five months to finish the book. Its cover is reddish with gold lettering. It has a colorful paper book jacket with a picture of Radha and Krishna in Goloka Vrindavan, along with Lord Chaitanya chanting in the spiritual world. On the inside flap, Bhaktivedanta Swami explains both the meaning of the front cover and the purpose of the *Srimad-Bhagavatam*.

Bhaktivedanta Swami presents his book to important people, many of whom often write favorable reviews. He also visits colleges and libraries and receives many orders. After a few years, and much hard work, Bhaktivedanta Swami is able to print three volumes of *Srimad-Bhagavatam*.

It is 1965, and Bhaktivedanta Swami is now sixty-nine years old. Scholars all over India know his books. He feels it is time to travel to America, but he needs to find a way to get there.

Bhaktivedanta Swami knows a devotee named Sumati Morarji, who once gave him a donation to print *Srimad-Bhagavatam*. Since she owns a steamship company, Bhaktivedanta Swami decides to again ask for her help. He explains that he needs a ticket to the United States on one of her ships.

Sumati Morarji is concerned. "Swamiji, you are so old to take such a risk. Do you think it is all right?"

Bhaktivedanta Swami is confident. "Do you know what my secretaries think?" she asks. "They say, 'Swamiji is going to die there.'"

Because she thinks that the voyage, and then life in a foreign country, will be too difficult for him, Sumati Morarji does not want to send Bhaktivedanta Swami to America. But he is determined. He convinces her that everything will be all right. After all, he has been preparing for this journey for many years.

Sumati Morarji finally agrees and asks her secretary, Mr. Choksi, to take Bhaktivedanta Swami shopping. If he is going to America, he will need warm clothes.

Mr. Choksi asks him, "Why do you want to go to the United States now that you are old?"

"I will be able to do something good, I am sure," he replies.

Sumati Morarji gives Bhaktivedanta Swami a ticket to travel on the Jaladuta, one of her cargo ships. It sails for America from Calcutta on August 13, 1965. He gets ready for his voyage.

On August 13, a friend named Mr. Bhattacarya hires a taxi to bring Bhaktivedanta Swami to the cargo ship. The ship's sailors watch as the two friends say goodbye on the dock below. Then Bhaktivedanta Swami walks alone up the gangway onto the deck of the Jaladuta.

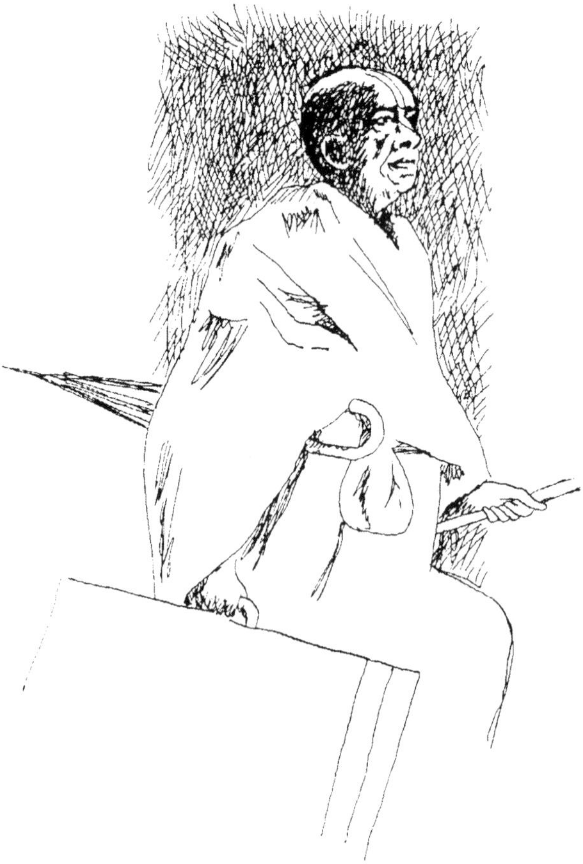

14

Coming to America

Although the Jaladuta is a cargo ship, it has a passenger cabin where Bhaktivedanta Swami can stay. The ship's captain is named Arun Pandia, and his wife is travelling with him. Sumati Morarji instructs them both to take good care of Bhaktivedanta Swami.

The ship sails across the Indian Ocean, then up the Red Sea. Unfortunately, Bhaktivedanta Swami begins to feel seasick, and along with headaches, dizziness, and vomiting, he also begins to feel severe pains in his chest. Within two days he suffers two heart attacks. He thinks that he may not live.

Then he has a dream in which Lord Krishna is rowing a boat, telling him not to be afraid. Krishna assures him that he should continue on to America. Bhaktivedanta Swami feels encouraged that Krishna is there to protect him. The heart attacks stop and he begins to feel better.

After two weeks at sea, the ship docks at Port Said, Egypt, near the Suez Canal. Captain Pandia and Bhaktivedanta Swami spend the day touring the city.

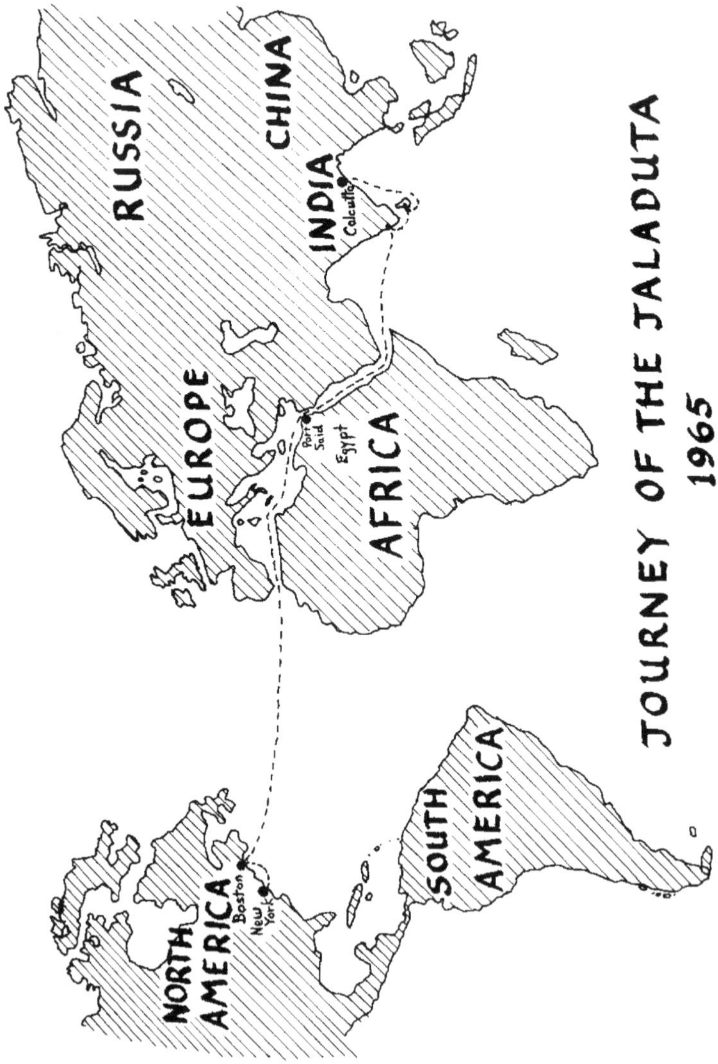
RUSSIA
CHINA
INDIA
Calcutta
EUROPE
AFRICA
Port Said
Egypt
NORTH AMERICA
Boston
New York
SOUTH AMERICA
JOURNEY OF THE JALADUTA
1965

After sailing the Mediterranean Sea, the Jaladuta begins to cross the vast Atlantic Ocean. Amazingly, there are no storms on this part of the voyage, and Captain Pandia tells his saintly guest that he has never seen such a calm Atlantic crossing. Bhaktivedanta Swami feels that Krishna is protecting the ship. If they had experienced the usual ocean storms, he thinks perhaps he would have died. He is still regaining his strength after two heart attacks on the Red Sea.

After thirty-five days, the Jaladuta arrives in the United States, at Boston Harbor. It is very early in the morning when the ship docks at Commonwealth Pier.

One of the first things Bhaktivedanta Swami sees in America are the letters "A&P" (the name of a supermarket) painted on the side of a warehouse. Among the piers there are ocean liners, fishing boats, lobster stands, and drab warehouses. He can also see in the distance the tall buildings of the Boston skyline.

Captain Pandia invites Bhaktivedanta Swami to join him on a walk through this historic American city. Together they pass among the waterfront warehouses until they reach a footbridge that takes them over a busy highway into Boston's downtown section. As they walk among the office towers, nightclubs, restaurants, stores, and old churches, the city gradually awakens to begin the day.

While Boston is an important American city, both wealthy and proud, Bhaktivedanta Swami feels that these people are striving after the wrong things. The happiness they seek will never satisfy their hearts as long as they are determined to forget their relationship with Krishna. Without God in the center, their success will prove bitter and false.

For much of his life, Bhaktivedanta Swami has waited for a chance to fulfill Srila Bhaktisiddhanta Sarasvati's dream of bringing Krishna consciousness to the proud Western nations. But now he wonders how these people will ever understand the message of Lord Chaitanya. He feels very small. He is not sure what he will be able to do by himself, all alone.

When he returns to his cabin aboard the Jaladuta, Bhaktivedanta Swami sits down and writes a poem in Bengali. He calls it "Markine Bhagavata Dharma" ("Teaching Krishna Consciousness in America"). This is part of his poem:

> My dear Lord Krishna, You are so kind upon this useless soul, but I do not know why You have brought me here. Now You can do whatever You like with me.
>
> How will they understand the mellows of devotional service? O Lord, I am simply praying for Your mercy so I can convince them about Your message.
>
> I wish that You may deliver them. Therefore if You so desire their deliverance, then only will they be able to understand Your message.
>
> Somehow or other, O Lord, You have brought me here to speak about You. Now, my Lord, it is up to You to make me a success or failure, as You like.
>
> O Lord, I am just a puppet in Your hands, so if You have brought me here to dance, then make me dance, make me dance, O Lord, make me dance as You like.
>
> signed, the most unfortunate, insignificant beggar,
> A. C. Bhaktivedanta Swami,
> On board the ship Jaladuta, Commonwealth Pier,
> Boston, Massachusetts, U.S.A.
> Dated 18th September, 1965.

Two days later, the Jaladuta reaches New York City. As the ship sails past the Statue of Liberty, Bhaktivedanta Swami views the Empire State Building and the other towering skyscrapers of the New York City skyline.

As he gets off the ship, Bhaktivedanta Swami isn't sure where to go. Fortunately, someone is supposed to meet him.

Back in India, a friend named Mr. Agarwal promised he would tell his son living in America to take care of Bhaktivedanta Swami when he arrives. The Agarwals, who live in Pennsylvania, arrange for a man to help Bhaktivedanta Swami find the bus that will take him to their home. Dressed as an Indian *sannyasi* in orange robes, carrying a small suitcase and umbrella, Bhaktivedanta Swami makes his way through New York City's busy streets to find the bus station.

As his bus pulls out beneath the shadow of the soaring skyscrapers, it heads for the Lincoln Tunnel, which goes under the Hudson River to New Jersey. Then the bus travels along the New Jersey Turnpike past seemingly endless fields of oil tanks, factories, and warehouses. Behind in the distance are the New York skyscrapers, and to the right are the jet airplanes at the Newark Airport. Along the side of the highway are huge steel towers carrying miles of electric power lines, and billboard after billboard advertising everything imaginable. It is an amazing sight. Of course, Bhaktivedanta Swami has seen big cities and factories in India, but he has never seen anything like this.

While America's industrial might is impressive, Bhaktivedanta Swami feels compassion. These people are determined to find happiness in material life, but in the end such happiness leaves the heart feeling painfully empty.

As the bus gets closer to Pennsylvania, the scenery gradually changes to countryside. It is almost midnight when Bhaktivedanta Swami arrives in Pittsburgh. There Mr. Agarwal's son, Gopal, is waiting to drive Bhaktivedanta Swami to his home in Butler, about an hour away. Gopal Agarwal respectfully folds his palms and bows, saying, "Welcome, Swamiji."

15

A Newcomer To a New Land

The Agarwals and their two young children live in a small house in Butler, Pennsylvania. Sally Agarwal, who grew up in the United States, met her Indian husband in America, where he was working as an engineer. They are both friendly people, but because their home is small, they rent a room down the street where Bhaktivedanta Swami can sleep at night.

Since it is unusual to have a Vaishnava *sannyasi* as a guest in Butler, Sally thinks people will be interested to learn about the Swami. She brings him to the local newspaper, the *Butler Eagle,* and they agree to write a story. They print a picture of Bhaktivedanta Swami holding open a *Srimad-Bhagavatam,* and they write that the *Bhagavatam* is like the Bible. They describe Bhaktivedanta Swami as a "learned teacher."

In the article Bhaktivedanta Swami explains, "My mission is to revive people's God consciousness. God is the father of all living beings in thousands of different forms." He suggests, "If Americans would give more attention to their spiritual life, they would be much happier."

Sally likes the Swami. At his request, she invites friends to her home in the evening for philosophical conversations.

Sally describes: "It was quite an intellectual group we were in, and they were fascinated by him. . . . This was just like a dream out of a book. Who would expect to meet a swami in someone's living room in Butler? It was really tremendous. . . . All the people liked him. . . . He was the easiest guest I ever had in my life, because when I couldn't spend time with him he chanted, and I knew he was perfectly happy."

While visiting Butler, the Swami wakes up early. At around seven in the morning, he walks the six or seven blocks from his rented room to the Agarwals' apartment. For breakfast he eats a bowl of cereal with milk—the same cereal he brought with him from India. Later in the morning he begins cooking lunch in the Agarwals' kitchen. While the Swami cooks, Sally works around the house and takes care of the children.

Sally remembers: "He was cooking this great big lunch which was ready at about eleven-thirty, and Gopal always came home for lunch around twelve. I used to serve Gopal a sandwich, and then he would go back to work. But it didn't take me long to realize that the food the Swami was cooking we'd enjoy too, so he started cooking that noon meal for all of us. Oh, and we'd enjoy it so much.

"Our fun was to show him what we knew of America. It was such fun to take him to the supermarket. He loved opening the package of okra or frozen beans, and he didn't have to clean them and cut them and do all those things. He opened the freezer everyday and just chose his items. It was fun to watch him. . . .

"So every day he'd have this big feast, and everything was great fun. We really enjoyed it. I would help him cut the things. He would spice it, and we would laugh. He was the most enjoyable man."

After lunch, Bhaktivedanta Swami walks back to his room. He returns in the evening and speaks at the Agarwals' home to guests until nine-thirty. Then Mr. Agarwal drives him back to his room for the night.

Sally had other memories of Swamiji staying at her home: "Our boy, Brij, was six or seven months old when the Swami came, and the Indians love boys. The Swami liked Brij. He was there when Brij first stood. The first time Brij made the attempt and actually succeeded, the Swami stood up and clapped. It was a celebration.

"One time something happened with our little girl, Pamela, who was only three years old. I used to take her to Sunday school, and she learned about Jesus in Sunday school. Then when she would see Swamiji with his robes on and everything, she would call him Swami Jesus. And this one time when it first dawned on us what she was saying, Swami smiled and said, 'And a little child shall lead them.' It was so funny."

During his stay with the Agarwals, Bhaktivedanta Swami learns a lot about life in America. He also gets a chance to speak about Krishna consciousness, both at the Agarwals' and also at a few local colleges, churches, and other groups. He gains confidence and wants to try preaching in a big city like New York.

Sally remembers: "After a month I really loved the Swami. I felt protective in a way, and he wanted to go. He was just going to New York, and then there was no one. I just couldn't imagine."

16

New York City

Through a friend, Bhaktivedanta Swami meets a man in New York City named Dr. Ramamurti Mishra. Dr. Mishra invites Bhaktivedanta Swami to stay at his apartment.

Dr. Mishra also has a yoga school close by, where he teaches his students the impersonal idea that everyone is God. But Bhaktivedanta Swami understands things differently; he realizes that Krishna is God. Although as individuals we may be small, our loving relationship with the Supreme Lord is wonderful and unlimited. Though the two teachers disagree on many important spiritual understandings, Bhaktivedanta Swami is a friendly and polite guest.

After a few weeks, the Swami moves to a room in the yoga school. There he spends most of his time translating scripture and typing manuscripts of his devotional books. Sometimes, if there is a yoga class, Dr. Mishra asks Bhaktivedanta Swami to lead a Hare Krishna *kirtan* for the students.

Every morning the Swami wakes up early, takes a bath, chants Hare Krishna on his beads, and works on his translations. Then he walks to Dr. Mishra's apartment to cook *prasadam*. Often Dr. Mishra joins him for breakfast.

The neighborhood is filled with tall buildings, shops, and restaurants. Sometimes the Swami walks to nearby Riverside Park, by the Hudson River. Often on weekends, Dr. Mishra brings Bhaktivedanta Swami and his yoga students to a spiritual retreat in the country.

Although Dr. Mishra and the Swami disagree on many things, they still become good friends. Dr. Mishra enjoys the Swami's cooking and chanting.

Dr. Mishra remembers: "I have never seen or met any devotee who sang so much, and his *kirtan* was just ambrosial. If you pay attention and become relaxed, that voice has a very electrical vibration on your heart. You cannot avoid it. Ninety-nine percent of the students got up and danced and chanted. And I felt blessed to meet such a great soul."

Since Dr. Mishra doesn't allow Bhaktivedanta Swami to give classes about Krishna consciousness at the yoga school, the Swami spends his time selling *Srimad-Bhagavatams* to the local bookstores.

In January of 1966, Bhaktivedanta Swami sees his first snowstorm. When he looks out the window at the building across the street, it appears so white that he thinks someone has painted it. Not only is there snow, but the temperature drops to ten degrees. Still, the Swami continues his daily walks.

Bhaktivedanta Swami writes letters to people he knows in India, asking them to help him start a Krishna temple in New York City. Although his Godbrothers agree that Krishna consciousness is needed in the West, they are unable to help. Fortunately, Bhaktivedanta Swami is not easily discouraged.

In February, the Swami moves from his room at Dr. Mishra's yoga school to an office downstairs. While at the yoga school he could talk only in private about Krishna consciousness, here he can give classes to the public. He still goes to Dr. Mishra's apartment to cook and take care of his personal needs.

Bhaktivedanta Swami begins giving classes on Mondays, Wednesdays, and Fridays. Although many of the students from the yoga school are curious to hear more from the Swami, soon new people also begin to come, and some of them seem much more than just curious.

A small New York cafe named the Paradox is a popular place for young people interested in spiritual and cultural improvement. News about the Swami reaches the Paradox crowd. Two friends, Harvey Cohen and Bill Epstein, like what Bhaktivedanta Swami is doing and tell everyone at the Paradox all about him. Now many young people begin visiting the Swami to hear him chant the Hare Krishna mantra and speak about *Bhagavad-gita*.

17

The Bowery

The Swami's new place is quite small. One day while he is out, someone breaks into his room and steals his tape recorder and typewriter. He decides that he again needs to move.

Harvey and Bill tell him that the young people mostly live downtown. Since Harvey is leaving for California, he invites the Swami to move into his downtown apartment. It is in the Bowery, a part of New York City.

The Bowery is famous as a place where drunks and homeless bums roam and live in the streets. While it is not a pleasant part of the city, Harvey's apartment is large. Another boy, named David Allen, also lives there and will help pay the rent. The Swami decides to move in.

The apartment has a large, open space with sunlight pouring in through both of the windows and a skylight overhead. In the corner is a kitchen and a bathroom. At the other end, a screen separates an area where the Swami can set up an office to do his translation work.

While there isn't much furniture in the apartment, there are rugs on the hardwood floors, and an old-fashioned table and raised platform where the Swami can sit and give lectures. A large picture of Lord Chaitanya stands on a wooden easel.

News of the Swami now living in the Bowery spreads quickly, particularly at the Paradox. His *kirtans* are especially popular, and many young musicians and artists want to hear the Swami sing the mystical Hare Krishna mantra.

The Swami gives a *Srimad-Bhagavatam* class every morning. David Allen, his roommate, as well as Robert Nelson and others regularly attend. Sometimes they also hold a cooking class. Bhaktivedanta Swami always has time for visitors. One new friend is Carl Yeargens. He likes Indian religion and music, and he wants to learn Sanskrit.

The Swami continues to give evening *Bhagavad-gita* classes on Mondays, Wednesdays, and Fridays. He speaks from the platform while his guests sit on pillows and mats on the floor. The room fills with the sweet smell of burning incense.

His new musician friends feel that the chanting is a mystical experience. The Swami teaches them about the importance of sound, and how simply by hearing they can develop God realization.

Sometimes while Bhaktivedanta Swami chants he plays a harmonium, a small hand-pumped organ. Other times he plays a drum while his guests play *kartals*. The Swami teaches them how to play them properly.

The evening class begins at eight o'clock. Everyone chants together for half an hour before Bhaktivedanta Swami speaks. Afterwards he answers questions and then chants again. The evening program usually ends by ten o'clock.

While the Swami's new students enjoy chanting Hare Krishna, they are not very interested in Krishna consciousness as a way of life. Still, Bhaktivedanta Swami offers them lessons from the *Bhagavad-gita*. He explains, "Krishna is the Supreme Consciousness, and Arjuna is asked to cooperate with the Supreme. Then he will be free from birth, death, old age, and disease."

Ideas about expanding consciousness are popular in America. The Swami explains how Krishna consciousness is the perfect consciousness.

It is now spring, and on his early morning walks Bhaktivedanta Swami carries an umbrella in case it rains. In the Bowery, most of the broken-down buildings are four or five stories tall. There are few trees, but many signs and billboards. On a clear day, one can see the top of the Empire State Building, thirty blocks away.

It is quiet in the early morning as he walks through the local neighborhoods, admiring different buildings and imagining how they could serve as temples. He also shops at nearby Chinese grocery stores for cooking ingredients, and sometimes the Swami's new friends go with him.

One friend, Jan, remembers the Swami on a morning walk: "I would see him among all the people down there, walking down the street. He always had an umbrella, and he would always have such a peaceful look on his face. He would just be walking along, sometimes stepping over the drunks. And I would get sort of nervous when I would meet him on the sidewalk. He would say, 'Are you chanting?' and I would say, 'Sometimes.' And then he would say, 'That's a good girl.'"

That spring, a reporter and photographer from *The Village Voice* visits the Swami to interview him and take photographs. *The Village Voice* is a popular newspaper among the young people.

The reporter, Howard Smith, remembers the Swami well. "I thought his ideas had a good chance of spreading because they seemed so practical. His head didn't seem to be in the clouds. He wasn't talking mysticism every other word. I guess that is where his soul was at, but that isn't where his normal conversational consciousness was at.

"It was obvious to me that I was not talking to some fellow who had just decided that he had seen God and was going to tell people about it. He seemed to be an educated man, much more than myself, actually. And I liked his humbleness. I just plain liked the guy.

"He explained everything I wanted to know—the importance of what he was wearing, the mark on his forehead, the bead bag. And I liked all his explanations. Everything was very practical. Then he talked about temples all over the world, and he said, 'Well, we have a long way to go. But I am very patient.'"

Things are going well for Bhaktivedanta Swami in the Bowery. Many young Americans appear interested in the chanting and attending his classes. But David, his roommate, still experiments with LSD. Because of the drug, David sometimes acts crazily. One day, after a bad LSD "trip," David begins running around the apartment moaning, yelling, and howling.

Carl Yeargens recalled: "He just flipped out, and the Swami had to deal with a crazy man. He was a crazy kid who always took too much."

This is not the friendly David the Swami knows as a roommate, but a wild-eyed madman. Bhaktivedanta Swami decides he needs to move out—now!

18

A New Start On Second Avenue

Bhaktivedanta Swami feels shocked as he walks alone on the Bowery streets. It certainly isn't safe anymore living with David. He could call his friend Dr. Mishra, but moving back to the yoga school would mean ending his evening *Bhagavad-gita* classes.

He decides to call Carl Yeargens, who at once agrees to let Bhaktivedanta Swami stay at his apartment. Carl lives close by and comes right over to help. After bringing the Swami to his apartment, Carl and Bill Epstein return to the Bowery to get some of his belongings. They find David there, calmer now, but still acting crazily from the LSD.

At Carl's place, the Swami continues holding *kirtans* and classes with his regular guests, but it is not the best place for meetings. The apartment is small and Carl's wife is not very interested in Indian culture. She is definitely not interested in turning her home into a temple. Though Carl wants to help the Swami, he doesn't want to disturb his wife. It's obvious they need to find Bhaktivedanta Swami a place of his own to start a Krishna conscious temple.

Carl and another friend, Michael Grant, look for a new place. Mike is good at getting things done, and he quickly finds a small storefront for rent on Second Avenue. He calls the owner and arranges to see it. He invites Carl and the Swami to come with him.

Mike meets Mr. Gardiner, the real estate agent, at the storefront. There is a sign hanging over the front window saying "Matchless Gifts." Mr. Gardiner tells them how recently this storefront had been used as a gift shop.

Mike explains how Bhaktivedanta Swami is an important author and scholar from India. When the Swami and Carl arrive, Mr. Gardiner brings everyone inside.

The empty storefront is plain and needs repainting, but it's big enough for meetings and doesn't cost much. Out the back door, Mr. Gardiner shows them a courtyard with trees and shrubs. Surrounding the courtyard are apartments, and one of them is empty. The group goes up a staircase to the second floor. There they see a small apartment where the Swami can live.

Bhaktivedanta Swami feels that this is a good place. Rent for both the apartment and storefront comes to $196. Carl and Mike agree to raise money for the first month's rent. Mr. Gardiner says he will need a week to repaint the apartment, and Carl and Mike also need time to get the money together.

Next week the Swami is ready to move in to his new place, and a number of friends meet him outside his old apartment in the Bowery. Everyone goes upstairs and finds something to carry. As they carry the Swami's belongings down the street, they look a bit like a safari caravan. Since it is the end of June, the summer sun makes their expedition to Second Avenue a hot one.

Second Avenue is a busy street filled with delivery trucks, taxis, and automobiles. Across the street from the storefront are shops and a small restaurant. Next door stands a huge, nine-story warehouse, and on the other side is a busy gas station on a large corner lot.

While the Swami's storefront isn't fancy, it is the best place yet. At the Paradox, Bill spreads the news of the Swami's new home.

19

The First Hare Krishna Temple in America

26 Second Avenue is in a part of New York called the Lower East Side. Also living among the neighborhood's poor Eastern European and Puerto Rican immigrants are a new group known as hippies.

The hippies are mostly young people from the middle-class suburbs outside the city. Their parents have good jobs and plenty of whatever money can buy. But for the hippies, money and buying things are not enough. They are looking for something more, and they are willing to give up everything they know in order to find it.

While the hippies feel that there must be more to life, they aren't sure exactly what it is or where to look for it. Many search for life's meaning through music, philosophy, drugs, and romance. In 1966, thousands of these young people are moving to New York City's Lower East Side, looking for something new. These are the first Westerners to take the Swami's message to heart.

Many hippies visit the Swami's neighborhood storefront. If ever someone meets him walking down the street, the Swami invites him to attend his classes. Others walk by the storefront and see a picture of Lord Chaitanya hanging in the window. Underneath, a sign tells them what time the classes are held. Many also hear about Bhaktivedanta Swami at the Paradox.

Some of the new visitors share an apartment together, close by on Mott Street. They recently returned from a trip to India, where they had hoped to find a spiritual guru. While walking along Second Avenue, Howard Wheeler is the first of the three roommates to meet the Swami.

Howard remembers: "After crossing the Bowery just before Second Avenue, I saw Swamiji strolling down the sidewalk, his head held high in the air, his hand in his bead bag. He struck me like a famous actor in a very familiar movie. He seemed ageless."

Bhaktivedanta Swami notices Howard as well, and they stop to talk. Howard asks the first question that comes to his mind: "Are you from India?"

Swamiji smiles, "Oh yes, and you?"

Howard says no, but he tells the Swami how he had just been there. After their conversation, Howard rushes home to tell his two roommates, Keith and Wally, about Bhaktivedanta Swami.

The Mott Street group also tell another friend, Chuck Barnett. Others, like Stephen Guarino, see the sign in the window and decide to come in. While new people want to hear what Bhaktivedanta Swami has to say about Krishna consciousness, as on the Bowery many others also come seeking something mystical in the chanting of the Hare Krishna mantra.

At the storefront, Prabhupada gives classes and encourages his guests to chant:

"And the transcendental vibration, Hare Krishna, will help us by cleaning the dust from the mirror of the mind. . . . So this process, the vibration of the transcendental sound—Hare Krishna, Hare Krishna, Krishna Krishna, Hare Hare/Hare Rama, Hare Rama, Rama Rama, Hare Hare—will cleanse the dust. And as soon as the dust is cleared, then, as you see your nice face in the mirror, similarly you can see your real constitutional position as spirit soul. . . . So, it doesn't matter what a person was doing before, what sinful activities. A person may not be perfect at first, but if he is engaged in service, then he will be purified."

Suddenly, in the middle of class, a drunken Bowery bum enters the storefront, whistling and shouting. The drunken man says, "How are ya? I'll be right back. I brought another thing."

Bhaktivedanta Swami replies, "Don't disturb. Sit down. We are talking seriously."

The drunken man says, "I'll put it up there. In a church? All right. I'll be right back."

The man has white hair and a short grizzly beard. His dirty clothes smell up the temple. As he leaves, the Swami chuckles softly and continues his lecture, but a few minutes later the bum returns and says, "How are ya?"

He is carrying something as he drunkenly tries to make his way to the back of the room. He opens the bathroom door, puts two rolls of toilet paper inside, and closes it. Next, he heads for a sink on the side of the room and puts some paper towels underneath it. Finally, he turns and stands before the Swami and his audience.

Bhaktivedanta Swami looks at him and asks, "What is this?"

The bum is silent.

Then the Swami begins to laugh. He thanks his visitor, who is now moving toward the door.

"Thank you. Thank you very much."

The bum leaves.

"Just see," Bhaktivedanta Swami tells his listeners. "It is a natural tendency to give some service. He is not in order, but he thought that 'Here is something, let me give some service.' Just see how automatically it comes. This is natural."

The young people in the audience look at one another. The whole experience is wonderful—first the Hare Krishna chanting with the Swami who looks like Buddha, then chanting and talking about

Krishna, and now finally this crazy bum. But Swamiji is calm and cool. He just sits on the floor and speaks about Krishna. He seems prepared for anything.

Sometimes Bhaktivedanta Swami asks his guests, who are only beginners in spiritual life, to dedicate themselves to preaching Krishna consciousness. He cannot wait for them to understand everything before he sends them out to preach—Krishna consciousness is just too important. The world needs Krishna conscious preachers now.

The Swami tells them in class: "People are suffering for want of Krishna consciousness. Therefore, each and every one of us should be engaged in the preaching work of Krishna consciousness for the benefit of the whole world. Lord Chaitanya, whose picture is in the front of our store, has very nicely preached the philosophy of Krishna consciousness. The Lord says, 'Just take my orders, all of you, and become a spiritual master.' Lord Chaitanya gives the order that in every country, you go and preach Krishna consciousness. So if we take up this missionary work to preach *Bhagavad-gita* as it is, without interpretation and without any material motives behind it—as it is—then Krishna says it shall be done."

At the end of the evening class Swamiji chants some more. Then around nine o'clock, a boy brings Bhaktivedanta Swami an apple along with a small wooden bowl and a knife. Most of the audience sits quietly, experiencing the aftereffects of the chanting. The Swami cuts the apple in half, and then in half again, gradually slicing all the fruit into the small bowl. He takes a piece and pops it into his mouth, then asks the boy to pass the rest to his guests. In this way Bhaktivedanta Swami makes certain everyone gets a chance to honor Krishna-*prasadam*.

20

The Swami's First Followers

The Swami decides to legally register his band of devotees. In July of 1966, Bhaktivedanta Swami's group becomes officially known as the International Society for Krishna Consciousness, or ISKCON.

A few of the Swami's followers move into the storefront. Keith from the Mott Street crowd becomes his first full-time helper. Every day for lunch, Keith begins cooking rice, *dal, sabji,* and chapatis. He also cleans the Swami's apartment.

Many of the Swami's other students, like Howard, Chuck, Steve, and Wally, also come to his apartment in the morning for a special *Bhagavad-gita* class. Since it is held very early, they chant softly so as not to disturb the neighbors. For each of them, spending time with the Swami is the most important part of their day.

Steve remembers: "Swamiji mentioned that mangoes were the king of all fruits, and he even mentioned that they were not easily available in this country. It occurred to me that I could bring him mangoes. Every day after work, I would purchase one nice mango and bring it to the Swamiji."

Wally recalled: "Some of the boys would say, 'I'm doing this for the Swami.' So I went to him and said, 'Is there something I can do for you?' He told me I could take notes in his class."

The boys feel that Swamiji is their direct connection to Krishna, and therefore their service to him is something special.

Although everyone calls the storefront "the temple," it is practically empty—it has no decorations. Howard, Keith, and Wally decide to brighten it up with posters, paintings, incense burners, and other decorations they brought back from India. They also bring their apartment curtains, which they had washed and dyed purple.

They place a large Oriental rug on the floor and hang the curtains on the back wall. In front of the curtains, they build a raised platform with a cushion for the Swami to sit on while he chants and gives class. Behind the platform they mount a large, circular picture of Radharani and Krishna. On the other walls they hang pictures of Lord Chaitanya and Hanuman.

As everyone wants to surprise the Swami, they keep the decorations a secret. In the evening, when he walks in for class, the devotees remain quiet while he examines the newly decorated temple. Swamiji then looks at the devotees and smiles broadly.

"You are advancing," he says. "Yes, this is Krishna consciousness."

He moves toward the platform. Everyone holds his breath, hoping the platform will hold Swamiji safely. Bhaktivedanta Swami sits down comfortably and begins to chant. He again looks around the storefront temple with a serious expression, and then smiles in appreciation of all their hard work. Everyone's heart fills with joy.

Michael Grant remembers what it was like in the newly decorated temple: "I came one evening, and all of a sudden there were carpets on the floor, pictures on the wall, and paintings. Just all of a sudden it had blossomed and was full of people. I was amazed how in just a matter of days, people had brought so many wonderful things. When I came that evening and saw how it had been decorated, then I wasn't so much worried that he was going to make it. I thought it was really beginning to take hold now."

The summer of 1966 brings happy days for the Swami. Not only are these young people attracted, but many more are seriously chanting Hare Krishna and performing devotional service. They may not always understand everything clearly, but they are enthusiastic. Bhaktivedanta Swami sees Krishna guiding them within their hearts toward spiritual life.

Everyday the Swami makes sure there is enough lunch *prasadam* for at least a dozen guests. When everything is ready, Swamiji washes his hands and mouth in the bathroom before he comes into the front room, where he stands by a low table in front of a picture of Lord Chaitanya. Keith brings out a large tray with stacks of chapatis, and pots of rice, *dal*, and *sabji*, and places them on the altar table. Everyone bows down with Swamiji as he says the Vaishnava prayers for offering food to Krishna.

Bhaktivedanta Swami sits with his young friends as they enjoy *prasadam*. He says that everyone should eat as much as possible. There is a happy family feeling among the new devotees. If someone isn't eating heartily, Swamiji calls the person's name and says, "Why are you not eating? Take *prasadam*." Then he laughs. On Sundays, he sometimes cooks a feast with special Indian dishes.

Steve remembers: "Swamiji personally cooked the *prasadam* and then served it to us upstairs in the front room of his apartment. We all sat in rows, and I remember him walking up and down in between the rows of boys, passing before us with his bare feet and serving us with a spoon from different pots. He would ask what we wanted—did we want more? And he would serve us with pleasure. These dishes were not ordinary, but sweets and savories—like sweet rice and *kachauris*—with special tastes. Even after we had all taken a full plate, he would come back and ask us to take more."

21

Initiations

One day, while Bhaktivedanta Swami and Keith are cooking in the kitchen, Keith suddenly asks, "Swami, could I become your disciple?"

"Yes," Swamiji replies, "Your name will be Krishna dasa."

Of course, there is more to initiation than getting a Sanskrit name, but this is the first time anyone asks. Soon the Swami announces that he will hold an initiation ceremony.

"What's initiation, Swamiji?" one of the boys asks.

Bhaktivedanta Swami replies, "I will tell you later."

But he does tell the boys that they will need *japa* beads for chanting. They go to a local store and buy large red beads and some cord for stringing them on. The Swami shows them how to do it.

While stringing their *japa* beads in the temple courtyard, the boys discuss what initiation could mean.

Wally says, "It's just a formality. You accept Swamiji as your spiritual master."

Howard asks, "What does that mean?"

Wally replies, "Nobody's very sure. In India it's a standard practice. Don't you think you want to take him as a spiritual master?"

Howard looks thoughtfully and says, "I don't know. He would seem to be a good spiritual master—whatever that is. I mean, I like him and his teachings a lot, so I guess in a way he's already my spiritual master. I just don't understand how it would change anything."

Wally says, "Neither do I. I guess it doesn't. It's just a formality."

On Janmastami, a few days later, Bhaktivedanta Swami tells the boys at the end of class, "Now I will tell you what is meant by initiation. Initiation means that the spiritual master accepts the student and agrees to take charge, and the student accepts the spiritual master and agrees to worship him as God." He pauses. "Any questions?"

No one speaks. The Swami then gets up and walks out of the room.

The devotees are stunned. For weeks Bhaktivedanta Swami has taught them that anyone who claims he is God is actually behaving more like a dog.

"My mind's just been blown," says Wally.

"*Everybody's* mind is blown," Howard agrees. "Swamiji just dropped a bomb."

Together the boys discuss what the Swami just said, but they can't figure it out. Finally they decide that Howard and Wally should go to ask the Swami.

In the Swami's apartment, Howard asks, "Does what you told us this morning mean we are supposed to accept the spiritual master to be God?"

Initiations

Bhaktivedanta Swami calmly explains, "That means he is due the same respect as God, being God's representative."

"Then he is not God?"

"No," he explains, "God is God. The spiritual master is His representative. Therefore, he is as good as God because he can deliver God to the sincere disciple. Is that clear?"

It is.

The next day, Bhaktivedanta Swami begins making arrangements for the initiation ceremony. Everyone is curious because no one has ever seen anything like it before. Eleven devotees ask to become disciples.

In the middle of the room there is a square, medium-sized, brick platform filled with a mound of dirt. Around the mound are eleven bananas, a container of ghee, some sesame seeds, whole barley grains, colored powders, and a bundle of kindling wood.

The room fills as Bhaktivedanta Swami and the eleven candidates sit down around the brick platform. Outside in the hall, guests watch through the door.

The Swami asks everyone to chant while he begins the ceremony by lighting a handful of fragrant incense sticks. He purifies himself by sipping a spoonful of water from a small brass container, then asks the other devotees to do the same. Everyone chants the Sanskrit prayers along with him, and then there is a short lecture.

Bhaktivedanta Swami chants on the initiates' red *japa* beads one set at a time, which takes over an hour. When he is done, he calls each new disciple before him. First he shows him how to chant, and then gives him a spiritual name. Next, the devotee bows down and returns to his sitting place. Along with *japa* beads and a new name, each disciple receives neck beads, which the Swami calls "dog collars." He says that whoever wears these neck beads belongs to Krishna.

Howard's new spiritual name is Hayagriva; Wally becomes Umapati; Mike is Mukunda; and Jan's new name is Janaki.

Next, Bhaktivedanta Swami starts the sacrificial fire. He sprinkles the colored powders in special patterns on the mound of earth. After dipping the short pieces of wood in the ghee, he lights them with a burning candle. He then places the flaming wood neatly in a pile in the center of the mound.

Bhaktivedanta Swami mixes sesame seeds and barley with some ghee in a bowl and passes it among the devotees. Each person takes a small handful. The Swami chants Sanskrit prayers, and at the end of each prayer he asks the devotees to chant *svaha* three times. Every time they say *svaha*, the devotees toss a handful of seeds into the flames.

For about twenty minutes, Bhaktivedanta Swami chants prayers and builds the fire. Soon the room is hot. Each of the eleven new disciples places a banana in the fire. Smoke fills the room as the bananas smother the flames.

Now the ceremony is over. Bhaktivedanta Swami stands up and smiles broadly as he claps his hands and chants Hare Krishna. All the devotees join in, chanting and dancing joyfully.

As the smoke clears from the apartment, the Swami jokes, "There was so much smoke I thought they might have to call the fire brigade."

Bhaktivedanta Swami is happy. The fire sacrifice, the prayers, the initiation, and everyone chanting Hare Krishna has created an auspicious feeling. It appears that the seed of Krishna consciousness has been planted in the West.

Two weeks later, the Swami holds another initiation ceremony. This time Keith becomes Kirtanananda, Steve becomes Satsvarupa, Bruce becomes Brahmananda, and Chuck becomes Acyutananda. It is another festive day in the Swami's apartment, with another fire sacrifice, chanting, and a big feast.

22

Chanting Hare Krishna

For a gentleman in his seventies, the Swami is quite healthy and active. He is always teaching Krishna consciousness, smiling, and chanting Hare Krishna. Although he is happy with the success of the new temple, the Swami plans to do more.

One day he gathers his band of followers together and tells them he wants to take them to Washington Square Park, about a half a mile away. The boys aren't sure what to expect.

Arriving at the park, the Swami and his boys sit down on a patch of lawn. He takes out his brass hand cymbals and begins chanting the Hare Krishna mantra. At first his disciples are shy, but soon their singing is strong and confident.

One devotee remembers: "It was a marvelous thing, a marvelous experience that Swamiji brought upon me. Because it opened me up a great deal, and I overcame a certain shyness—the first time to chant out in the middle of everything."

A curious crowd gathers to watch. The Swami chants for half an hour while the crowd stays to listen. For his audience, the chanting has turned an ordinary stroll in the park into a special event. This is the first time in America that the chanting of Hare Krishna has been performed in public. Afterwards, while walking back to the temple, the Swami and his boys feel happy and victorious.

Soon Bhaktivedanta Swami tries the public chanting again, this time at Tompkin's Square Park. This park is crowded with hippies and others from the local neighborhood. There are lots of children and dogs running loose. A few of the devotees walking ahead spread out an Oriental carpet. They are already chanting when the Swami and his followers arrive from the temple. Bhaktivedanta Swami sits down on the rug, looks at his group, and smiles. Clapping his hands, Swamiji counts one , two , *three* . . . one, two, *three*. He wants the boys to play *kartals* to this beat, and he claps until they get it right.

Next, the Swami begins singing Sanskrit prayers that no one outside of India has ever heard before. While playing a small drum under a large oak tree with his group in the park, he sings these mysterious prayers describing the pure love experienced between Radha and Krishna. People gather to watch. Then the Swami begins chanting the *maha-mantra:* Hare Krishna, Hare Krishna, Krishna Krishna, Hare Hare/Hare Rama, Hare Rama, Rama Rama, Hare Hare. The devotees follow, but they chant in low, muddled voices. Bhaktivedanta Swami's singing remains clear and strong, and his followers get better each time.

A few of the hippies sit cross-legged along the edge of the rug. They listen, clap, and try to chant. Musicians in the park wander over, one by one. Gradually dozens join in playing metal and bamboo flutes, mouth organs, conga and bongo drums, saxophones, tambourines, and guitars. As more musicians come forward, the crowd grows larger, listening to Bhaktivedanta Swami and the devotees chanting Hare Krishna.

One musician remembers that day well: "The park resounded. The musicians were very careful to listen to the mantras. . . . I have talked to a couple of musicians about it, and we agreed that in his head this Swami must have had hundreds and hundreds of melodies that had been brought back from the other side of the world. . . . 'Hey,' they would say, 'listen to this holy monk.' People were really sure there were going to be unusual feats. . . . But when the simplicity of what the Swami was really saying, when you began to sense it—it turned you around."

The Swami motions to his disciples to get up and dance. Brahmananda and Acyutananda are the first to stand. With their arms raised up just like Lord Chaitanya, they face each other and begin dancing the "Swami step"—one foot crossing over, and then back, then the other foot doing the same. Photographers in the crowd take pictures.

And so it goes for hours. Somehow everyone's music blends together, but above it all everyone hears the Swami's chanting. At one point he stands up and gives a short lecture, and when he is finished he invites his audience back to the temple at 26 Second Avenue. Then he sits down and again leads the chanting.

Later, when the Swami and his boys return to the storefront, they find a large crowd waiting for them. These people want to hear more about the chanting and the elderly Swami, who along with his followers created a beautiful scene in the park.

The storefront fills, with more people standing outside hoping to get in. Swamiji walks through the crowd directly to the dais. He sits down before the largest crowd ever and begins speaking about Krishna. For Bhaktivedanta Swami, talking about Krishna consciousness is as natural as breathing.

It is late when the crowd begins to leave. The Swami goes upstairs to his apartment. One devotee suggests they chant like this every week in the park. Bhaktivedanta Swami says, "Every day."

The Swami lies down on his thin mat as he continues speaking to the few devotees still with him, but his voice gradually trails as he appears to doze off. Quietly, the boys tiptoe out of the apartment, softly shutting the door behind them.

23

The Hare Krishna Explosion

The next morning, two different newspapers report on the devotees' chanting in the park. One paper, *The New York Times*, is famous worldwide. Its article is titled "Swami's Flock Chants in Park to Find Ecstasy."

The other newspaper, *The East Village Other*, is popular among the hippies. On the front page is a photo of the Swami standing under the oak tree speaking to the crowd. Above the picture it says "Save Earth Now," and underneath is the Hare Krishna mantra. The Swami likes both articles.

Other local newspapers begin to report on the Swami and his followers. Even at the local clubs, musicians play the Hare Krishna melodies they hear in the park. Krishna consciousness is becoming popular on New York City's Lower East Side.

Meanwhile, Bhaktivedanta Swami teaches both Kirtanananda and Brahmananda to cook. He wants them to prepare a special feast on Sundays. On leaflets they pass out to other young people, the devotees advertise it as a "Love Feast." Brahmananda asks

Swamiji how he learned to cook so expertly. The Swami tells him that he learned by watching his mother.

At first there are only a handful of guests, but the devotees don't seem to mind. They keep themselves busy eating all the delicious *prasadam*. After a few weeks, however, so many guests attend that many have to sit in the courtyard outside, with their paper plates full of *prasadam*.

The Swami also wants to start printing *Back to Godhead* magazine. Brahmananda's brother, now called Gargamuni, finds a small printing press for sale. The Swami puts Hayagriva and another disciple in charge of making the magazine. In no time, the devotees are printing and selling *Back to Godhead*.

One day, a man from a local record company visits the temple. He likes the chanting and wants to make a record. The Swami likes the idea. Two weeks later, Bhaktivedanta Swami goes to the recording studio and records an album with his group, "The Hare Krishna Chanters."

Mukunda and his wife, Janaki, move to San Francisco to start a new temple. Around New Year's Day, they mail Bhaktivedanta Swami a letter explaining how they have found a storefront. They include a plane ticket so the Swami can visit.

Mukunda writes, "We are busy converting it into a temple now." He describes how thousands of hippies from all over the country are moving to San Francisco, especially to the neighborhood where the temple is located. When the Swami hears this he says, "I shall go immediately."

Many years later, Brahmananda recalled the Swami's new plan to leave New York:

"We were shocked that he was going to leave. I never thought that Krishna consciousness would go beyond the Lower East Side, what to speak of New York City. I thought that this was it, and it would stay here eternally."

Still, Bhaktivedanta Swami has plans to bring Krishna consciousness to everyone, everywhere. He is confident and determined. He is eager to travel and expand the chanting of the Hare Krishna *mahamantra*.

The boys arrange for a car to take Swamiji to the airport. It is a gray and cold day. Inside his apartment, steam hisses from the radiators. He carries only a suitcase—mostly clothes and some books. Kirtanananda will take care of the apartment while he is away.

Bhaktivedanta Swami feels happy about the success of the New York temple. It is a good start. Now with the help of his young disciples, he is ready to expand.

In San Francisco, Mukunda and Janaki greet Bhaktivedanta Swami at the airport. Some of the other New York devotees are also there, along with over fifty San Francisco hippies. Reporters interview the Swami at the airport. A report of his arrival is shown on the evening television news. The next day, two of the city's largest newspapers print stories.

Soon, Swamiji's young followers travel all over America and Europe starting new centers. Whenever they open a temple they invite the Swami to visit, and Bhaktivedanta Swami begins traveling all around the world inspiring people to become Krishna conscious.

One day, while in Boston, he mentions that traditionally a disciple calls his spiritual master by a more respectful name than Swamiji.

A devotee asks, "What should we call you?"

"A spiritual master is usually addressed by names like Gurudeva, Vishnupada, or Prabhupada," replies Bhaktivedanta Swami.

"May we call you Prabhupada?"

"Yes."

Many disciples are reluctant to change, for they have learned to love Bhaktivedanta Swami as "Swamiji." He tells them that they can still call him Swamiji if they want, but gradually all his disciples begin calling their spiritual master Srila Prabhupada.

Around this time, six devotees travel to London, England, to begin another new temple. Amazingly, they meet the Beatles, the most famous rock band in the history of popular music. The Beatles already know about the chanting, from listening to the Hare Krishna album Srila Prabhupada made with his disciples in New York. One member, George Harrison, is particularly attracted to Krishna consciousness. He helps the devotees make another record, and one of the songs becomes a hit in Europe. George also helps Srila Prabhupada print books, and he buys a large mansion in England for a Krishna temple that becomes known as Bhaktivedanta Manor.

Other devotees travel to India. Some begin farms around the world, where Vaishnavas can live simply and practice Krishna consciousness. They also start schools called *gurukulas*, where children can learn to grow up as devotees.

In India, Prabhupada begins huge temple projects in Vrindavan, Bombay, and Mayapur. Vrindavan is famous as the town where Krishna grew up, and

Bombay is India's richest city. Mayapur is the birthplace of Lord Chaitanya, and Srila Prabhupada has plans to build a city there. It will become the world headquarters for a worldwide Krishna consciousness movement.

Srila Prabhupada's disciples also begin printing his books. He has translated dozens of Vaishnava scriptures into English with explanations, called "Purports," to help the reader understand Krishna consciousness. The devotees start their own printing press called ISKCON Press. Later, when devotees around the world begin selling hundreds of thousands of books, large companies are hired to do the printing work.

Srila Prabhupada continues to travel, even to places like Africa, Australia, and Russia. Everywhere his disciples are opening temples, and they are finding thousands of people interested in Krishna consciousness. Prabhupada inspires and guides them.

In America, the devotees begin holding Rathayatra festivals, just like Srila Prabhupada did when he was a small boy in Calcutta. The first big festival is held in San Francisco, but soon there are festivals in many important cities around the world.

Led by Srila Prabhupada, his disciples bring Krishna consciousness to practically every country on the planet. This fulfills both the desire of Lord Chaitanya and of Srila Prabhupada's own spiritual master, Srila Bhaktisiddhanta Sarasvati. It is their ambition for all human beings to have a chance to chant the Hare Krishna mantra, to develop their relationship with Lord Krishna, and ultimately to go back home to their natural condition in the spiritual world.

Now it is 1977, and Srila Prabhupada is eighty-one years old. It has been twelve years since he first left

India for America aboard the Jaladuta. Since then, the Hare Krishna movement has grown all over the world. Now there are over one hundred ISKCON temples, as well as farms, *gurukulas*, restaurants, and dozens of different Vaishnava books being distributed by the millions to people around the globe.

In the fall of 1977, Srila Prabhupada's health is not good. He becomes so ill that his disciples need to carry him on a palanquin. During this time he lives in Vrindavan in a small apartment at ISKCON's Krishna-Balaram temple, built especially for him by the devotees. Although he needs to stay in bed, he still teaches Krishna consciousness. With the help of a tape recorder, he continues translating books about devotional service.

Eventually there comes a time for everyone who has accepted a material body to leave both it and this world behind. At the time of death, our body breaks down and the soul can no longer stay. This is not an easy experience, for while living in our body we usually become attached to everything associated with it. Thus, how to die as a devotee of God is the final, most important lesson that Srila Prabupada must teach his disciples. He has already taught them how to live in Krishna consciousness. Now he teaches them how to leave this world thinking of Krishna, in love.

As Srila Prabhupada's body becomes weaker, his disciples understand that their spiritual master is preparing to leave. It is a sad and difficult thought. He tells them that they can pray, "My dear Lord Krishna, if You so desire, please cure Srila Prabhupada." He says everything depends on Krishna. However, his disciples begin to feel that Lord Krishna wants their spiritual master to come back home to Him in the spiritual world.

During this time, loving disciples from around the world surround Srila Prabhupada. They gather by his bed to be with him during his final moments. Their tears flow as they chant Hare Krishna with hearts full of love.

Since Srila Prabhupada has spent his entire life thinking about and serving Krishna with love, surely his heart's desire carries him back home to his Lord. On November 14, 1977, at seven-thirty in the evening, Srila Prabhupada teaches his followers that final lesson: how to leave this world remembering Krishna, and thus go home to live with Him eternally in complete knowledge and happiness.

But then, many deeply consider how Srila Prabhupada remains with us—in his books, through his teachings, and by his life's example. For his followers he left hundreds of centers where devotees can associate together and learn how to enter more deeply into their own relationship with Lord Sri Krishna.

Whatever success Srila Prabhupada achieved, he understood it to be the blessing of his own spiritual master, Srila Bhaktisiddhanta Sarasvati. As a faithful disciple, Srila Prabhupada followed his spiritual master's example and teachings with full love and devotion. By his own example, he taught his followers how to experience complete success in Krishna consciousness. That was the unique offering of His Divine Grace Abhay Caranaravinda Bhaktivedanta Swami Prabhupada. Through his deep sincerity and honest devotion, he presented to the world the pure gift of Krishna consciousness in a way that had never been done before.

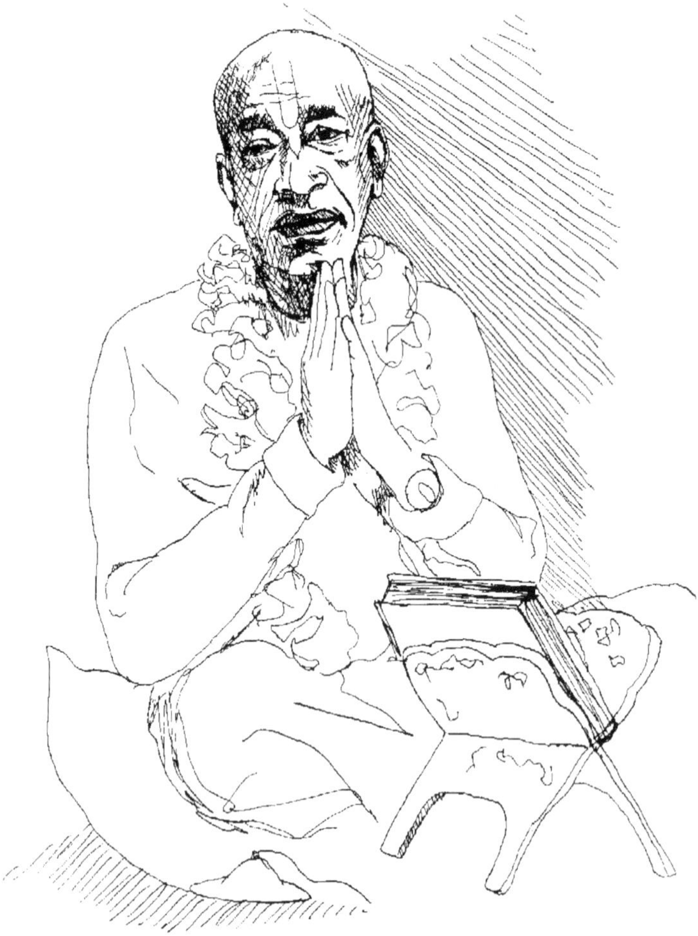

24

Prabhupada's Victory
By Kalakantha dasa

Come, my children, and hear the tale
Of Prabhupada's victory, and how he sailed
Alone to challenge the godless West
And give the world Krishna consciousness.

In old Calcutta, under British rule,
Our young Abhay was fresh from school,
Dressed in *khadi*, and newly wed.
"Come meet this sadhu," his best friend said.

Bhaktisiddhanta, straight and tall,
Promptly spoke (he never stalled):
"Take your Western education;
Preach for Krishna in Western nations!"

Abhay replied, "But who will listen,
When India is ruled by Britain?
His guru said, "No ruling state
Can make Chaitanya's movement wait."

Capturing his guru's vision,
Abhay took up Chaitanya's mission.
Forty years then hurried by.
A swami now, the day arrived

When standing on a weathered dock,
He caught a boat and turned his back
On all familiar things he'd known,
His friends and his Vrindavan home.

On rolling sea, in tiny berth,
No place to stand on solid earth,
His stomach failed and then his heart.
Would journey's end come at its start?

The man quite small, the sea gigantic,
But Krishna calmed the harsh Atlantic,
Carrying this precious soul
As Matsya bore the Vedic scrolls.

What was to come, no one could tell,
For one who ventured straight to hell
To speak what his guru had spoken,
Disciplic chain to stay unbroken.

In Boston Bay he wrote a poem:
"Lord Krishna, I am far from home.
For you, My Lord, I take this chance.
Now kindly make your puppet dance."

First to suburbs, then to town,
To Bowery bums sprawled on the ground,
To roommate mad on LSD,
The Swami went on fearlessly.

Beneath a massive, spreading oak,
The humble swami boldly spoke:
"Free yourself from *maya's* pain,
By chanting Krishna's holy name."

Listening were a precious few.
First came one, and then came two
To join the Swami's unaided voice,
To chant the Name and then rejoice

In tasting food he called *prasad*,
Encountering a personal God,
Relishing the *kirtan's* beat,
Sitting at the Swami's feet.

They rode with him to spiritual heights
And spent such blissful days and nights
That happily they gave up sin,
And vowed to not take birth again.

The Swami gave these youthful hearts
Temples, schools, and farms to start,
And books to print for BBT
To benedict humanity.

Chanting, dancing, madness cured,
Growing saintly, calm, and pure,
His students called him Prabhupada:
"Servant at the feet of God."

Like Vamanadev of giant steps,
Prabhupada flew East and West.
To India he brought his men
To make the Indians proud again.

Teaching what Chaitanya taught
Bhakti for all, Brahman for naught
Complete with potent references
To the *Gita As It Is*.

His followers from foreign nations
Caused an Indian sensation.
Projects sprung up by the score,
The largest in Sri Mayapur.

In just ten years he spanned the world!
The ISKCON banner he unfurled
Flew high and proud in every nation,
His books sold in local translation.

His teachings not to be ignored,
He turned the faithless to the Lord,
Installing Krishna's Deity,
To serve with pomp and purity.

None could equal his success
Promoting Krishna consciousness.
Completing his great victory,
He went to Krishna's lotus feet.

Prabhupada said, though all must die,
We'll find ISKCON in the spiritual sky.
Prabhupada is there, and Krishna too
I'd love to join them—wouldn't you?

GLOSSARY

Advaita Acharya — a great devotee of Lord Chaitanya who helped spread the glories of chanting the Hare Krishna maha-mantra.

Artik — a ceremony for worshiping the Lord. It's often performed on the temple altar before the Deities. The *pujari* offers incense, ghee lamp, flowers, and a peacock fan to the Deities.

BBT — stands for "Bhaktivedanta Book Trust." It is a company set up by Srila Prabhupada responsible for printing his books.

Bhagavad-gita — means "the song of God." It is a book that was originally spoken by Krishna to His friend Arjuna. It explains all about the science of Krishna consciousness.

Bhakti — devotional service to Lord Krishna.

Brahmana — an intelligent scholar or priest in Vedic society.

Chapati — a whole wheat flat bread similar to a tortilla.

Chaitanya-charitamrita — a long book describing the life and philosophy of Lord Chaitanya.

Dal — a spicy, bean soup.

Deities — forms of the Supreme Personality of Godhead that often look like beautiful statues. These forms are authorized by the Vedic literatures for the devotees to worship. Krishna says in the Vedas that He appears as the Deities.

The devotees have Deities of Radharani and Krishna, or Lord Chaitanya and Lord Nityananda, on the altar in most of their temples.

Dhoti — a cloth that is worn around the waist and legs by men and boys. It is often seen worn in India.

Garuda — giant, eagle-like carrier of Lord Vishnu. He is considered a great devotee.

Ghee — a cooking oil made from purified butter.

Goloka Vrindavan — the highest planet in the spiritual world, where Krishna personally resides.

Hare Krishna maha-mantra — holy names of Krishna chanted as a prayer to enter into devotional service to God. Also called "the great chant of deliverance."

Harinam — chanting of the holy names of the Lord together in a group.

Janmastami — the festival celebrating Lord Krishna's birthday.

Japa beads — the beads devotees use when chanting by themselves.

Kachauri — a fried pastry stuffed with fried *dal* beans.

Khadi — a type of cloth used in making Indian style clothing.

Kartals — small, brass hand cymbals.

Kirtan — chanting about the Supreme Lord, often by singing before the Deities.

Glossary

Krishna — an intimate name of the Supreme Personality of Godhead. It means "all-attractive."

Krishna consciousness — the realization or experience of one's eternal relationship with Krishna, or God.

Kurta — long shirt worn by boys and men. It is often seen in India.

Lord Chaitanya — Krishna, when he appeared as a devotee. He taught the chanting of the holy names, and started the Hare Krishna movement 500 years ago in India.

Lord Jagannatha — means "Lord of the Universe," and refers to a Deity of Lord Krishna.

Mahabharata — an ancient story describing the activities of great saints and heroes during Vedic times. At its climax, Lord Krishna speaks the *Bhagavad-gita*.

Mridanga — a special drum used by devotees for kirtan. It has two drum heads, one on each end.

Parikram — a walking tour of holy places.

Prasadam — food offered to and blessed by Krishna.

Pujari — a devotee priest who takes care of the Deities.

Radharani — Lord Krishna's closest and dearest friend. She is His eternal consort. If a devotee wants to make Krishna happy, he must first become a loving servant of Radharani.

Ramayana — an ancient story describing the pastimes of Vishnu, or Krishna, as the great king Lord Ramachandra.

Sabji — a main vegetable dish.
Sadhu — a saintly person.
Sannyasi — a person in the renounced order.
Sari — a cotton or silk dress-like wrap worn by women.
Srimad-Bhagavatam — means "the beautiful story of the pastimes of the Supreme Personality of Godhead." This book is very long, and it is divided into twelve parts, called cantos. It describes Krishna in some of His incarnations, like Lord Ramachandra, and it also describes the lives of many great devotees.
Swami — one able to control his senses. A person in the renounced order.

Vaishnava — a devotee of Vishnu or Krishna.
Vedas — the four original Vedic scriptures. Veda also means "knowledge."
Vedic culture — the culture based on the Vedas.

Made in the USA
Columbia, SC
07 August 2017